W9-DAL-812

AS GOOD AS GOLD

RECIPES CELEBRATING **50** YEARS OF FOOD AND FAMILY

Holy Innocents' Episcopal School Fine Arts Alliance

Atlanta, Georgia

Holy Innocents' Episcopal School Fine Arts Alliance
805 Mt. Vernon Highway NW
Atlanta, GA 30327

Leah Hopkins Henry
Cover Art and Design

Fran Milner
Graphic Assistance

Proceeds from the sale of this book will be used to support the
Fine Arts Department with a portion going to our sister school in Haiti.

Copyright © 2008

ISBN: 978-0-9816775-0-7

First Printing   2008   3,000 copies

To order: www.hies.org

WIMMER
COOKBOOKS

A CONSOLIDATED GRAPHICS COMPANY

800.548.2537   wimmerco.com

HIES MISSION STATEMENT

Holy Innocents' Episcopal School develops in students a love of learning, respect for self and others, faith in God, and a sense of service to the world community.

HOLY INNOCENTS' FINE ARTS ALLIANCE MISSION STATEMENT

To promote and support the Fine Arts Department of Holy Innocents' Episcopal School, recognizing the importance in the creative development of the whole child.

COOKBOOK COMMITTEE

Nora Borne	Maggie McMullen
Leah Henry	Barb Meyer
Carol Luther	Susan Sapronov

FINE ARTS ALLIANCE EXECUTIVE BOARD

President	Nora Borne
Vice President	Leah Henry
Secretary	Mary Bev Barrett
Treasurer	Catherine Bennett
Faculty Liaison	Phyllis Gray
Hospitality	Alexis Vear
President Emeritus	Susan Sapronov

DEDICATION

This 50th Anniversary Cookbook is dedicated to all past and present members of the HIES community. With God's grace, we have come to this school each day for the past 50 years to educate our children and prepare them for an honest and productive life.

HISTORY OF HOLY INNOCENTS' EPISCOPAL SCHOOL

1872   The history of the school is rooted in that of Holy Innocents' Episcopal Church. The name was chosen in memory of the innocent children caught in Herod's rage.

1955   Five acres of land where Holy Innocents' now stands were purchased from Mrs. James L Riley, with an additional 2.8 acres bought a year later.

1959   Holy Innocents' Parish Day School was founded.

1967   A new pre-school facility was completed.

1968   The school became incorporated as Holy Innocents' Parish Day School and a Board of Trustees was established.

1970   The name of the school was changed to Holy Innocents' Episcopal School.

1978   Motor Activities Center (MAC) was completed.

1981   Eight acres of land were purchased from Life of Georgia.

1983   A new Middle School facility was constructed and a computer lab was added.

1988   Fine Arts Center was completed. Holy Innocents' Episcopal School acquired James L Riley Elementary School.

1989   The Upper School was approved.

1991   The first ninth grade class was enrolled.

1993   A new gymnasium for the Middle and Upper School was completed.

1994   The first senior class was enrolled with graduation scheduled for May 29, 1995.

1995   First graduating class of the Upper School.

1998   The Alan A. Lewis Pre-School was dedicated in memory of former student, Alan A. Lewis.

2005   Razing of MAC (Motor Activities Center) for construction of new Middle School. New Middle School Building named Rowan Family Middle School. New South Campus athletic fields connected to Main Campus by tunnel under Mount Vernon Hwy. State of the art gymnasium completed.

2006   Rowan Family Middle School opens.

2007   Lower School renamed and dedicated Dorothy Sullivan Lower School. Statement and revised philosophy approved by Board.

Heads of School

1959   Lillabel West - Director

1962   Barbara Chambers - Principal

1965   Elliott Galloway - Headmaster

1969   Dr. J. Russell Frank - Headmaster

1974   Alice L. Malcom - Interim Headmaster

1975   Del R. Coggins - Headmaster

1983   Alice L. Malcom - Headmaster

1996   Dr. Susan R. Grosbeck - Head of School

2003   Kirk R. Duncan - Head of School

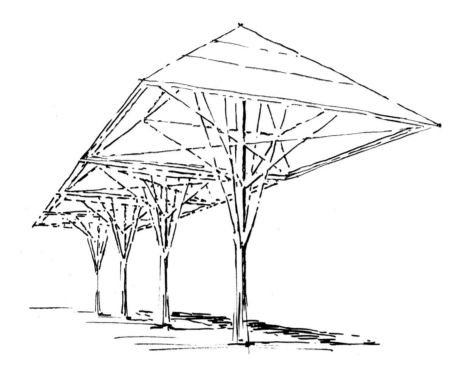

"When the new high school was being built, we needed a drop off in front of the building. Whatever the design, my objective was to keep it lighthearted. The Trees of Knowledge canopies were the result. It was not my intent to name them but they soon became commonly known as the "Trees of Knowledge" as they resembled trees.

It was a personal treat for me to be selected to convert Riley Elementary to the new high school. More projects followed including the gymnasium, preschool and Middle School library. My family has been involved with Holy Innocents' since our children were baptized here over 40 years ago. Now it is with great pride to see my grandchildren baptized here and attend the school as our children did. I am honored to be involved in the past, present and now the future of Holy Innocents'."

THOMAS W. VENTULETT, III

HOLY INNOCENTS' ALMA MATER — 1976

WORDS AND MUSIC BY JIM JEFFERS

1. A school was born and so was formed just a few years ago
    Where people walk the halls with smiles that set your heart a glow.
    A friendly place to seek the truth and try to understand
    A way of life and brotherhood that lends a helping hand.

    Chorus: Father teach us to love
    Follow us day by day,
    Give us peace and good will,
    And help us find your way.

2. We seek the knowledge of the world in books and people's minds,
    And hope to build anew our world, supporting all mankind.
    To give ourselves to others, and better friend to be,
    We'll build a stronger union that binds you to me.

    Chorus

3. Time moves on and people go reaching for a star.
    The things they've learned from our school will take them mighty far.
    So give the future what you have and never look behind,
    Remember Holy Innocents' and to its name be kind.

    Chorus

HOLY INNOCENTS' EPISCOPAL SCHOOL SONG

WORDS AND MUSIC BY JOHN PAUL WALTERS

Holy Innocents', Home of the golden bear, Arms that hold us close

Hearts that truly care Holy Innocents' building body and soul;

Instilling confidence, bidding us to grow. Holy, Holy, Holy

Innocents' You have given us the knowledge that we need to succeed
in the world and make it a better place for the human race with God's

Gift of grace Holy Innocents' Bless these bonds we share love that lifts us up

Hearts that truly care Holy Innocents' Golden Bears

Help Us, O God, Each Day to Know

Help us, O God, each day to know your presence through created things
when crickets chirp, or soft winds blow in fresh-cut grass where sweet dew clings,
but most of all your love we find in people honest, true, and kind.

In every person may we learn to recognize some special worth
to lay aside the world's concern with looks or wealth or place of birth,
to move beyond what may seem odd and find within a child of God.

Enlarge our sense of what can be: inspire each mind and fire each heart
to set imagination free, raise strength to skill, and nourish art:
yet may all gifts be understood as valued for the common good.

So teach us how to love the truth that we may seek it all our days:
sustain the eagerness of youth with wisdom's strength through life's long maze.
And when our search, O God, is done, show us that you and truth are one.

Prayer of Thanksgiving
BY REV. JEFF REICHMANN
CURRENT HEAD CHAPLAIN
HOLY INNOCENTS' EPISCOPAL SCHOOL

Almighty God, we give thanks for the many blessings we enjoy, especially the meals you provide. You nourish and give us life. Through your bounty we are bound to one another and joyfully celebrate all that we have. We pray we will always be mindful of those less fortunate, especially the poor, the hungry and all those who seek our prayers, for in giving us life we make your love and presence known. All this we ask in your Holy Name. Amen.

TABLE OF CONTENTS

H SPECIAL HOLY INNOCENTS' CONTRIBUTOR   KID FRIENDLY   HEART HEALTHY

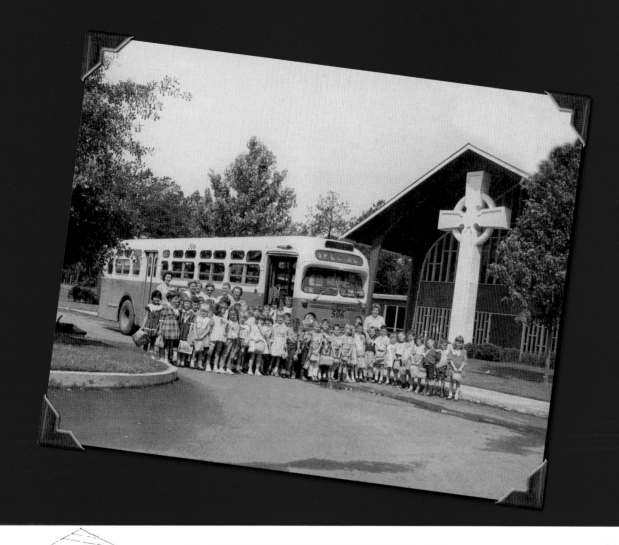

APPETIZERS AND BEVERAGES

ASPARAGUS AND GRUYÈRE TART

Black pepper and sour cream
pastry dough, see recipe
3 pounds thick white or
green asparagus, trimmed to
6 inches and peeled

Kosher salt to taste
1 cup heavy cream
2 large eggs
½ teaspoon kosher salt

¼ teaspoon grated nutmeg
Pepper to taste
1 cup finely grated Gruyère
cheese

Roll out pastry dough on a floured surface into a 15½ inch round. Transfer to pizza pan. Trim edge just enough to make even. Fold edge over and pinch to form a ½ inch high double thick side. Pierce bottom of shell with fork. Refrigerate at least 30 minutes.

Line shell with foil. Fill with pie weights or raw rice. Bake at 375 degrees 20 minutes until sides are firm. Remove foil and weights. Bake an additional 10 minutes until golden browned. Cool.

Layer asparagus on steamer rack, sprinkling each layer with salt. Cover and steam about 8 minutes for green asparagus or 12 minutes for white asparagus. Plunge asparagus in bowl of ice water. Drain well and pat dry with paper towels. Whisk together cream, eggs, salt and nutmeg. Add pepper. Pour custard evenly over tart crust.

Top with two-thirds Gruyère cheese. Arrange asparagus in custard with tips out like the spokes of a wheel. Sprinkle remaining Gruyère cheese on top. Bake 20 minutes or until custard is set. Broil 2-3 inches from heat source 1-2 minutes until golden browned.

SERVES 12-15

May substitute a 12 inch tart pan for pizza pan and trim asparagus to 5½ inch pieces.

Black Pepper and Sour Cream Pastry Dough

2¼ cups all-purpose flour
1 teaspoon salt
¾ teaspoon pepper

⅛ teaspoon sugar
1¼ sticks cold unsalted butter,
  cut into pieces

⅓ cup cold vegetable shortening
3 tablespoons sour cream
3 tablespoons ice water

Blend together flour, salt, pepper, sugar, butter and shortening with fingertips or pastry blender until it resemble coarse meal. Combine sour cream and water. Stir into dough with a fork until incorporated. Shape dough into a ball.

Flatten dough into a 6 inch square on lightly floured surface. Roll out dough into a roughly 18 x 6 inch rectangle. Fold into thirds to form a 6 inch square. Turn dough so open-ended side is near. Roll out to 18 x 6 inch rectangle again. Dust work surface with flour. Fold into thirds again. Repeat rolling and folding one more time. Wrap dough in plastic wrap and refrigerate at least 1 hour.

SERVES 12-15

Baked Vidalia Onion Dip

2 tablespoons butter
3 large Vidalia onions, coarsely
  chopped
1 package (8 ounce) shredded
  Swiss cheese

2 cups mayonnaise
1 can (8 ounce) sliced water
  chestnuts, drained and chopped
¼ cup dry white wine

1 garlic clove, minced
½ teaspoon Tabasco sauce
Tortilla chips or crackers

Melt butter in a large skillet over medium-high heat. Sauté onions 10 minutes or until tender. Combine Swiss cheese, mayonnaise, water chestnuts, wine, garlic and Tabasco. Mix well. Stir in onions until blended. Spoon mixture into a lightly greased 2 quart baking dish. Bake at 375 degrees 25 minutes. Let stand 10 minutes. Serve with tortilla chips or crackers.

SERVES 8-10

AVOCADO AND SMOKED SALMON MOUSSE

8 ounces thinly sliced smoked
    salmon

1 package (8 ounce) cream cheese,
    softened

1 cup sour cream

1 teaspoon hot pepper sauce

¼ teaspoon salt

2 tablespoons lemon juice

1 teaspoon unflavored gelatin

½ cup minced green onions

1 large ripe avocado, peeled, pitted
    and thinly sliced

1 jar (5 ounce) salmon roe

Toasted croutons or crackers

Line a 4 cup round mold with plastic wrap. Layer one-third salmon over wrap, overlapping slices and hanging slices over mold edges. Chop remaining salmon into ½ inch pieces and set aside. Beat cream cheese and sour cream with electric mixer until smooth. Stir in pepper sauce and salt. Heat lemon juice in a small saucepan over very low heat. Pour into a ½ cup ramekin. Sprinkle gelatin on top, stirring to dissolve. Pour gelatin into cream cheese mixture. Fold in chopped salmon and green onions.

Spoon one-third mousse into mold. Top with a layer avocado slices. Gently spread with one-half roe. Spread one-third mousse over roe. Top with remaining avocado and roe. Spread remaining mousse on top. Fold overhanging salmon over to completely cover mousse. Cover mold with plastic wrap. Refrigerate about 3 hours until firm.

Place mold in a bowl of warm water 10 seconds. Unwrap plastic wrap and invert onto a serving platter. Gently shake to release mold. Remove bottom plastic wrap. Serve with toasted croutons or crackers.

SERVES 20

♥ BLACK BEAN SALSA

¾ package (10 ounce) frozen white
  corn, thawed
½ bunch green onion, chopped
1 can (15 ounce) black beans, rinsed

1 sweet red or yellow pepper,
  chopped
½ cup chopped cilantro
¼ cup balsamic vinegar

¼ cup olive oil
¼ teaspoon ground cumin
Salt and pepper to taste
Tortilla chips

Combine corn, green onions, black beans, peppers, cilantro, vinegar, oil, cumin, salt and pepper. Mix well. Refrigerate until ready to serve. Serve with tortilla chips.

SERVES 12

May add 1 pint cherry tomatoes, diced and 1 ripe avocado, chopped.

BRIE WITH PESTO AND SUN-DRIED TOMATOES

¾ cup sun-dried tomatoes
2 garlic cloves, minced
3 tablespoons minced parsley

2-4 tablespoons olive oil
1 wheel (2 pound) Brie cheese
3 tablespoons basil pesto

Parsley sprigs for garnish
Assorted crackers

Reconstitute sun-dried tomatoes by covering with boiling water. Soak 3 minutes. Drain and finely chop. Add garlic, parsley and enough olive oil to moisten. Remove rind from top of Brie cheese, leaving a 1¼ inch border of rind around edge. Spoon pesto over cut Brie. Spread tomato mixture on top. Garnish with parsley sprigs. Serve at room temperature with crackers.

SERVES 12-15

BRUSCHETTA WITH
FRISÉE, PROSCIUTTO AND MOZZARELLA

1 baguette, cut on the diagonal into 18½ inch slices
3 tablespoons olive oil

18 paper-thin slices prosciutto
1 ball (8 ounce) mozzarella, cut into 18 thin slices

1 head frisée leaves, separated
2 tablespoons red wine vinaigrette

Arrange bread slices on 1-2 large baking sheets. Brush with olive oil. Bake at 375 degrees 10-15 minutes until crostini are crisp and pale golden browned.

Place one slice prosciutto on work surface. Layer cheese slice and 2-3 frisée leaves on top, allowing tops to protrude from one end. Roll prosciutto around cheese and frisée. Place on toasted bread. Arrange crostini on platter. Drizzle with vinaigrette and serve.

SERVES 6-8

CAVIAR PIE

2 packages (8 ounces each) cream cheese, softened
4 hard-cooked eggs

½ cup very finely chopped onions
2 jars black caviar

1 lemon, thinly sliced and curled
Toast rounds

Beat cream cheese until smooth. Press into bottom and up sides of 9 inch pie plate to form a crust. Refrigerate. Chop eggs with a fork until crumbly. Combine eggs and onions. Spoon over cream cheese crust. Gently spoon caviar over eggs, covering completely. Top with lemon curls. Serve with toast rounds.

SERVES 8-10

HH MRS. THOMAS W. VENTULETT, III
WIFE OF HIES ARCHITECT

BOURSIN CHEESE

2 packages (8 ounces each) cream
   cheese, softened
2 sticks unsalted butter, softened
2 garlic cloves, crushed

½ teaspoon dried oregano
¼ teaspoon dried basil
¼ teaspoon dried dill
¼ teaspoon dried marjoram

¼ teaspoon pepper
¼ teaspoon ground thyme
Assorted crackers

Blend cream cheese and butter in food processor until smooth. Add garlic, oregano, basil, dill, marjoram, pepper and thyme. Beat until well combined. Pack mixture in a container or crock. Refrigerate 12 hours before serving. Serve with crackers. Store in airtight container in refrigerator for several weeks. Do not freeze.

SERVES 8-10

My sister-in-law makes this every year for all her friends. We always look forward to it. It makes a great hostess gift combined with a package of crackers.

CHEESE WAFERS

2 sticks butter, softened
2½ cups grated sharp Cheddar
   cheese

⅓ cup powdered sugar
1¼ teaspoons salt
½ teaspoon cayenne pepper

½ cup pecans, chopped
2½ cups all-purpose flour

Cream butter and Cheddar cheese. Add powdered sugar, salt and cayenne. Mix well. Add pecans and flour. Roll mixture into several logs 2-2½ inches in diameter. Wrap logs in wax paper. Refrigerate. Cut into slices. Place on a greased baking sheet. Bake at 350 degrees 15-18 minutes until lightly browned.

SERVES 15-20

☀♡ CHICKEN SATAY WITH SPICY PEANUT SAUCE AND CUCUMBER RELISH

PEANUT SAUCE

1 cup coconut milk

3 tablespoons red curry paste

½ cup chunky peanut butter

½ cup chicken broth

¼ cup palm sugar or brown sugar

2 tablespoons tamarind liquid or lime juice

1 teaspoon salt

CUCUMBER RELISH

1 large Japanese cucumber, peeled, halved and thinly sliced

2 shallots, thinly sliced

1 small Thai chili or Serrano chili, thinly sliced

⅓ cup white vinegar

2 teaspoons palm sugar or brown sugar

1 teaspoon salt

Cilantro leaves for garnish

CHICKEN

½ cup coconut milk

1 tablespoon fish sauce

2 teaspoons red curry paste

1 teaspoon palm sugar or brown sugar

1 tablespoon chopped cilantro

½ teaspoon ground turmeric

Salt and pepper to taste

1 pound boneless skinless chicken breast halves

Bamboo skewers, soaked in cold water

PEANUT SAUCE

Bring coconut milk to simmer in small saucepan. Whisk in curry paste about 1-2 minutes until dissolved. Whisk in peanut butter, broth and sugar. Reduce heat and simmer 5 minutes, stirring constantly, until smooth. Remove from heat and add tamarind and salt. Set aside to cool to room temperature.

CUCUMBER RELISH

Combine cucumbers, shallots and chilies in a bowl. Heat vinegar, sugar and salt in a saucepan until boiling. Cook 3 minutes until sugar dissolves. Remove from heat. Cool to room temperature. Pour vinegar mixture over cucumber mixture. Garnish with cilantro leaves.

Chicken Satay with Spicy Peanut Sauce and Cucumber Relish, continued

CHICKEN

Combine coconut milk, fish sauce, curry paste, palm sugar, cilantro, turmeric, salt and pepper in a bowl. Slice chicken into 3 inch long and 1 inch wide strips. Add to marinade, turning to coat. Cover and refrigerate up to 4 hours. Thread chicken onto soaked bamboo skewers. Grill 5-7 minutes, turning once, until cooked through. Serve with peanut sauce and cucumber relish.

SERVES 4-6

COTTAGE TAPENADE

GARLIC CROSTINI
1 baguette

3-4 garlic cloves, crushed or pressed   Olive oil

TAPENADE
1 cup pitted black olives

1 cup pimento-stuffed green olives

1 large garlic clove, peeled

¼ cup flat-leaf parsley

1 tablespoon red wine vinegar

1 teaspoon lemon juice

¼ cup olive oil

Pepper to taste

GARLIC CROSTINI

Slice baguette on diagonal into ¼ inch slices. Blend garlic with oil. Brush bread with oil mixture. Broil about 2 minutes until lightly toasted.

TAPENADE

Combine black olives, green olives, garlic, parsley, vinegar and lemon juice in food processor. Pulse until mixture is evenly chopped. Add 2 tablespoons oil and pulse to combine. Add remaining oil and pulse until mixture become a fine paste. Add pepper. Serve with garlic crostini.

SERVES 1¼ CUPS

♡ COWBOY CAVIAR

1 teaspoon lime zest
½ cup lime juice
¼ cup olive oil
1 teaspoon brown sugar
1 teaspoon chili powder

½ teaspoon salt
½ teaspoon ground cumin
1 can (15 ounce) black beans
1 can (15 ounce) black-eyed peas

1½ cups frozen whole kernel corn, thawed
½ small bell pepper, chopped
⅓ cup chopped cilantro

Whisk together lime zest, lime juice, oil, brown sugar, chili powder, salt and cumin. Add black beans, black-eyed peas, corn, peppers and cilantro. Mix well. Refrigerate.

SERVES 12

CRAB AND ARTICHOKE DIP

1 package (8 ounce) cream cheese, softened
½ cup mayonnaise
Salt and pepper to taste
1 can (7 ounce) crabmeat, well drained

1 jar (6 ounce) marinated artichoke hearts, well drained and chopped
¼ cup sliced green onions
½ cup diced sweet red peppers
½ cup diced celery

¼ cup finely chopped parsley
1 teaspoon lemon juice
1 teaspoon Tabasco sauce
Crackers or baguette slices

Beat cream cheese in food processor until smooth. Add mayonnaise. In a separate bowl, combine salt, pepper, crabmeat, artichokes, green onions, peppers, celery, parsley, lemon juice and Tabasco. Mix well. Fold into cream cheese mixture. Mix well. Serve on crackers or baguette slices.

SERVES 12

PARSLEY RANCH DIP

1 cup sour cream
1 cup mayonnaise
3 garlic cloves

2 cups packed parsley, roughly chopped (1 bunch)

¼ cup roughly chopped chives
Salt and pepper to taste

Combine sour cream, mayonnaise, garlic, parsley, chives, salt and pepper in a food processor. Process until smooth and well blended. Transfer to a serving bowl. Cover and refrigerate at least 1 hour. Serve with cucumbers, carrots, green beans, sugar snap peas, jicama or tortilla chips.

SERVES 2¼ CUPS

Our bold spin on this much-loved classic features a hearty dose of parsley, which makes it lighter and more refreshing than traditional recipes. Consider mixing this one ahead of time. It tastes even better after one day of refrigeration.

CREAM CHEESE DIP

2 packages (8 ounces each) cream cheese, softened
1 package (1 ounce) dry ranch dressing mix

1 can (11 ounce) whole kernel corn, drained
1 can (4 ounce) chopped black olives, drained

1 can (4 ounce) chopped jalapeños or green chilies, drained
1 medium sweet red pepper, chopped
Corn or tortilla chips

Beat together cream cheese and dressing mix until smooth. Stir in corn, olives, jalapeños and peppers. Refrigerate at least 2 hours. Spoon out onto a serving plate and surround with corn or tortilla chips.

SERVES 15

FIESTA CORN DIP

2 cans (15 ounce) Mexican corn
1½ cups mayonnaise

1 package (8 ounce) shredded
   Colby Jack cheese
½ cup diced jalapeños or jar brand

1 cup grated Parmesan cheese
Scoop or regular corn chips

Combine corn, mayonnaise, Jack cheese, jalapeños and Parmesan cheese. Mix well. Pour mixture into a casserole dish. Bake at 350 degrees 25-30 minutes or until bubbly. Serve with scoop or regular corn chips.

SERVES 12

SEVEN LAYER MEXICAN DIP

1 can (8 ounce) refried beans
1 can Fritos bean dip
½ cup salsa
1 container (16 ounce) Dean
   guacamole dip

1 cup sour cream
½ cup mayonnaise
1 package (1½ ounce) taco
   seasoning mix

Shredded Jack and Cheddar
   cheese
1 can (4 ounce) sliced black olives
3 small tomatoes, chopped
2 bunches green onions, chopped

Combine refried beans, bean dip and salsa. Spread mixture on bottom of a small rectangular baking dish. Top with guacamole. Blend sour cream, mayonnaise and taco seasoning. Spread over guacamole. Top with layers of olives, tomatoes and green onions.

SERVES 6-8

May substitute 2 avocados, mashed with fork, and blended with juice of 1 lemon and salt for the store bought guacamole.

LILA'S GOAT CHEESE TORTE

1 log (7 ounce) goat cheese, softened

1 package (8 ounce) cream cheese, softened

2 tablespoons chopped sun-dried tomatoes

3 tablespoons fresh pesto

Line a small shallow bowl or ramekin with plastic wrap, overlapping the edges to cover torte. Cream goat cheese and cream cheese until smooth. Layer half tomatoes in bowl. Top with half cheese mixture. Spread with pesto and remaining tomatoes. Cover with remaining cheese mixture. May invert onto a serving dish.

SERVES 6

This is a delicious and colorful appetizer served with crackers. May layer cream cheese with cranberries and roasted pecans or try olive Tapenade.

GOAT CHEESE APPETIZER

2 small rolls goat cheese

1 package (1 ounce) dry pesto sauce mix

1 large jar (10 ounce) marinated sun-dried tomatoes, drained

Crostini or crackers

Microwave goat cheese in a pie plate 15 seconds until cheese melts. Spread over bottom of plate. Prepare pesto according to package directions. Pour over goat cheese. Spread tomatoes over pesto. Cover and refrigerate 2 hours. Serve with crostini or crackers.

SERVES 8-10

GOAT CHEESE AND SUN-DRIED TOMATO TARTINES

12 (½ inch) thick baguette slices
2 tablespoons extra-virgin olive oil
1 medium tomato, peeled, seeded and cut into ¼ inch dice
2 tablespoons julienned soft sun-dried tomatoes, not in oil

1 tablespoon torn fresh basil
1 teaspoon sherry vinegar
½ tablespoon extra-virgin olive oil
2 tablespoons bottled black olive Tapenade

1 log (8 ounce) soft mild goat cheese, cut into ½ inch thick slices
Salt and pepper to taste
½ tablespoon extra-virgin olive oil
Basil leaves, torn for garnish
½ tablespoon extra-virgin olive oil

Preheat oven to 350 degrees. Brush one side baguette slices with 2 tablespoons oil and arrange oil side up on a baking sheet. Toast bread about 7 minutes until golden browned. Transfer to a rack to cool. Combine tomatoes, sun-dried tomatoes, basil, vinegar and olive oil. Spread Tapenade over each baguette slice. Top with a goat cheese slice and rounded teaspoon tomato mixture. Arrange tartines on a baking sheet. Sprinkle with salt and pepper. Drizzle with olive oil. Bake about 5 minutes until cheese softens. Transfer to a serving platter. Garnish with basil leaves. Drizzle with olive oil.

SERVES 6

Toasts may be prepared 2 days in advance. Cool completely and store in an airtight container at room temperature. Tomato mixture may be prepared 1 day in advance. Cover and refrigerate.

RASPBERRY BRIE

Brie cheese	1 pint fresh raspberries	Crackers
Raspberry preserves	Sliced almonds	

Remove rind from Brie cheese and allow to reach room temperature. Microwave preserves for 1 minute. Pour preserves over Brie cheese. Top with fresh raspberries and almonds. Serve with crackers.

SERVES 8-10

GRAHAM'S BRIE EN CROÛTE

1 sheet frozen puff pastry	⅛ teaspoon cinnamon	1 egg, beaten
1 tablespoon unsalted butter	1 wheel (8 ounce) Brie cheese	Crackers
½ cup walnuts	¼ cup packed brown sugar	

Defrost pastry 15-20 minutes and unfold. Melt butter in a saucepan. Sauté walnuts 5 minutes until golden browned. Stir in cinnamon to coat walnuts. Spread walnut mixture over top of Brie cheese. Sprinkle with brown sugar. Lay pastry flat out. Place Brie cheese in center of pastry. Gather up edges of pastry and press on cheese, securing at the top. Gently squeeze together the excess dough and tie with kitchen twine. Brush top and sides with egg. Place on a baking sheet. Bake at 375 degrees 20 minutes or until golden browned.

SERVES 12

To give a special look, cut extra pastry into heart or flower shapes and bake until golden browned.

HOT CRAB DIP

1 package (8 ounce) cream cheese, softened

½ pound flaked crabmeat, fresh or canned

2 tablespoons crab juice

Dash of lemon juice

¼-½ teaspoon horseradish

2 tablespoons chopped onions

¼ teaspoon salt

⅛ teaspoon garlic powder

Combine cream cheese, crabmeat, crab juice, lemon juice, horseradish, onions, salt and garlic powder. Mix well. Place in a casserole dish. Refrigerate 1 hour. Bake at 375 degrees 15 minutes.

SERVES 8-10

JACK CHEESE "SALSA"

1 package (8 ounce) shredded Monterey Jack Cheese

1 package (8 ounce) shredded pepper Jack cheese

2 green onions, chopped

1 tomato, chopped

¼ cup cilantro, chopped

1 can (4 ounce) sliced black olives with jalapeños

1 can (4 ounce) chopped green chilies

Italian dressing

Tortilla chips

Combine Monterey Jack cheese, pepper Jack cheese, green onions, tomatoes, cilantro, black olives, green chilies and Italian dressing. Mix well. Serve with tortilla chips.

SERVES 10-12

HAM ROLLS

2 sticks butter, softened
3 tablespoons prepared mustard
3 tablespoons poppy seeds

1 teaspoon Worcestershire sauce
1 medium onion, finely chopped
1 pound minced ham

1 package (12 ounce) shredded
    Swiss cheese
3 packages party rolls

Cream butter, mustard, poppy seeds and Worcestershire sauce. Add onions, ham and Swiss cheese. Mix well. Slice rolls horizontally separating top from bottom. Spread ham mixture on bottom half of rolls. Replace top half. Bake at 400 degrees 10 minutes. Freezes well.

SERVES 12-15

HOT CHEESE HORS D'OEUVRES

2 eggs
3 tablespoons self-rising flour
Dash of salt
⅓ cup milk

1 package (8 ounce) shredded sharp
    Cheddar cheese
1 package (8 ounce) shredded hot
    jalapeño cheese

1 can (4 ounce) chopped jalapeño
    peppers, drained

Beat eggs. Stir in flour, salt and milk. Add Cheddar cheese, jalapeño cheese and peppers. Press mixture into a 9 x 9 x 2-inch baking dish (thick pieces) or 13 x 9 x 2-inch baking dish (thin pieces). Bake at 350 degrees 30 minutes until golden browned.

SERVES 8-12

 # HUMMUS

1 can (15½ ounce) chickpeas, rinsed	¼ cup water	Dash of cayenne pepper
¼ cup tahini	1 garlic clove, minced	3 tablespoons lemon juice
¼ cup extra virgin olive oil	¾ teaspoon salt	

Combine chickpeas, tahini, oil, water, garlic, salt, cayenne and lemon juice in a food processor. Blend until smooth.

SERVES 6-8

Tahini is sesame paste and can be found in the international aisle of the grocery store. Be sure to stir it thoroughly before measuring.

NAN NAN'S PIMENTO CHEESE SPREAD

1 cup grated sharp Cheddar cheese	2-3 tablespoons grated onions	1 cup mayonnaise
1 cup grated mild Cheddar cheese	1 tablespoon Worcestershire sauce	Dash of cayenne pepper
1 cup grated Monterey Jack cheese	1 tablespoon lemon juice	Salt and pepper to taste
1 jar (4 ounce) pimentos and liquid	2 tablespoons prepared mustard	

Combine sharp Cheddar cheese, mild Cheddar cheese, Jack cheese, pimentos and liquid, onions, Worcestershire sauce, lemon juice, mustard, mayonnaise, cayenne, salt and pepper. Mix well. Cover and refrigerate at least 1-2 hours.

SERVES 12-15

This spread may be stored in the refrigerator for 10 days.

This is my great Grandmother's pimento cheese recipe. Everyone loves this version. It is an easy summer appetizer served with crackers or as a sandwich spread made with sliced tomatoes and a piece of lettuce.

HEALTHY AND DELICIOUS TRAIL MIX

Unsalted peanuts
  (peanuts, cashews or almonds)
Sunflower seeds
Dried cranberries, cherries
  and apricots

Raisins
Mini semi-sweet chocolate chips
Mini pretzels

Multi grain Cheerios
Whole wheat Chex cereal
Granola

In a large bowl, combine ¼ cup of any of the eight ingredients of choice.

SERVES 4-6

NUTS AND BOLTS CHEX MIX

1 package (15 ounce) corn chex
1 package (15 ounce) rice chex
1 package (16 ounce) small stick
  pretzels

2 pounds pecans
2 sticks butter
2 sticks margarine
2 teaspoons garlic salt

1 tablespoon Worcestershire sauce
1 teaspoon chili powder
2 teaspoons celery salt
1 teaspoon red hot sauce

Combine corn cereal, rice cereal, pretzels and pecans in a large bowl. Melt butter and margarine in a saucepan. Add garlic salt, Worcestershire sauce, chili powder, celery salt and hot sauce. Pour butter mixture over dry ingredients. Toss to coat. Spread mixture onto a baking sheet. Bake at 200 degrees 2 hours, stirring occasionally.

SERVES 20

JOAN FARLEY'S SHRIMP DIP

1 package (8 ounce) cream cheese, softened

1 package (3 ounce) cream cheese, softened

1 lemon, juiced

½ cup mayonnaise

2 tablespoons ketchup

1 medium onion, grated

1 teaspoon Worcestershire sauce

¾ pound medium shrimp, cooked and peeled

Beat cream cheeses, lemon juice, mayonnaise, ketchup, onions and Worcestershire sauce with electric mixer until creamy. Add shrimp. Cover and refrigerate at least 3 hours.

SERVES 6-8

"BRUSHETTA" SALMON SPREAD

16 ounce white king salmon

1 package (8 ounce) cream cheese, softened

6 Roma tomatoes, diced

6 basil leaves, rolled together and snipped into ribbons

1 garlic clove, chopped

½ cup balsamic vinaigrette

½ lemon, juiced

Pinch of sea salt and pepper

Shredded Parmesan and Romano cheese

2 basil leaves

Place salmon on a serving plate. Spread cream cheese evenly over salmon, pressing down. Combine tomatoes, basil ribbons, garlic, vinaigrette, lemon juice, salt and pepper in a bowl. Mix until well blended. Spread tomato mixture over cream cheese. Sprinkle with Parmesan and Romano cheese. Garnish with basil leaves.

SERVES 10-12

This is what our family likes to have out for all holidays or just anytime.

PÂTÉ OF THE SOUTH
(CHEESE PIMENTO SPREAD)

2 packages (8 ounces each) shredded sharp Cheddar cheese

1 package (3 ounce) cream cheese, softened

½ cup mayonnaise

1 tablespoon grated onions

½ teaspoon cayenne pepper

1 jar (4 ounce) pimentos, drained

Crackers

Beat Cheddar cheese, cream cheese, mayonnaise, onions and cayenne with an electric mixer 3 minutes. Add pimentos. Beat until pimentos are shredded. Spoon mixture into a crock and refrigerate. Bring to room temperature before serving with crackers.

SERVES 8-10

 SALSA-BEAN DIP

4 green onions, cut into 1½ inch pieces

2 garlic cloves

½ teaspoon ground cumin

½ teaspoon salt

2 cans (15 ounce) cannelloni beans, rinsed and drained

¼ cup mayonnaise

¼ cup lemon juice

½ jar salsa

Cilantro for garnish

Tortilla chips

Combine green onions, garlic, cumin and salt in a food processor. Process until coarsely chopped. Add beans, mayonnaise and lemon juice. Process until smooth, scraping down sides occasionally. Spoon mixture into a shallow 9 inch baking dish. Process salsa in food processor until smooth. Spoon into center of bean mixture. Pull the point of a toothpick through salsa toward edge of dish to create a starburst design. Refrigerate or serve at room temperature with tortilla chips.

SERVES 8-10

PUFF PASTRY STRAWS

TOMATO BASIL SEASONING

¼ cup grated Parmesan cheese

2 tablespoons finely chopped sun-dried tomatoes in oil, drained

1 tablespoon minced garlic

1 teaspoon dried basil

PASTRY

1 sheet puff pastry, room temperature

1 large egg, beaten

1½ teaspoons coarse salt

TOMATO BASIL SEASONING

Combine Parmesan cheese, sun-dried tomatoes, garlic and basil in a small bowl.

PASTRY

Unfold pastry and lay flat on lightly floured surface. Roll out to 14 x 10 inch rectangle, ¹⁄₁₆ inch thick. Cut pastry in half crosswise. Lightly brush both halves with egg. Sprinkle tomato basil seasoning evenly on one-half pastry. Place second pastry half egg side down over seasoned half, aligning edges. Gently roll to seal edges without enlarging rectangle.

Cut rectangle lengthwise into ½ inch wide strips. Lightly brush tops with egg. Sprinkle with salt and press gently into pastry. One at a time, pick up strips by both ends, twist in opposite directions. Place 1½ inches apart on two buttered 15 x 12 baking sheets. Press ends onto sheets.

Bake straws at 400 degrees 8-13 minutes until crisp and lightly browned, switching pan positions halfway through baking. Let straws cool about 1 minute on sheets. Using a wide spatula, loosen straws while warm. Transfer to a rack. If straws stick, return briefly to oven to reheat. Serve warm or cool.

SERVES 8-10

SPICY CRAB DIP

1 package (8 ounce) cream cheese, softened
2 tablespoons mayonnaise
2 dashes of Worcestershire sauce
2 dashes of Tabasco sauce

Dash of hot pepper sauce
1-2 teaspoons horseradish
1 package frozen snow crabmeat, thawed or 6-10 ounces crabmeat, in pieces

Parmesan cheese
Paprika for garnish
Mild unsalted wafers

Blend cream cheese, mayonnaise, Worcestershire sauce, Tabasco, pepper sauce and horseradish. Mix well. Add crabmeat. Spread mixture into a 9 inch round pan. Generously sprinkle with Parmesan cheese. May refrigerate at this point. Garnish with paprika. Bake at 300 degrees 30 minutes. Serve with wafers.

SERVES 8-10

MARK GROESBECK
HUSBAND OF SUE GROESBECK, FORMER HIES HEADMASTER

SWISS-ALMOND DIP

½ cup sliced almonds
2 packages (8 ounces each) cream cheese, softened
⅔ cup mayonnaise

1 package (12 ounce) shredded Swiss cheese
¼ cup chopped green onions
2 dashes of ground nutmeg

Pepper to taste
Crackers, apple slices or bread slices

Toast almonds in a skillet until golden browned, shaking pan constantly. Beat together cream cheese and mayonnaise until smooth. Stir in Swiss cheese, green onions and almonds. Add nutmeg and pepper. Spread mixture into a 1 quart baking dish or 9 inch pie plate. Bake at 350 degrees 20 minutes until slightly browned. Serve with crackers, apple slices or bread slices.

SERVES 12

STEVE'S GREAT CHEESE DIP AKA JEANNIE'S OLD BOYFRIEND'S GREAT CHEESE DIP

1 pound ground beef
1 pound spicy sausage

1 package (2 pound) processed
   cheese loaf
1 can (10¾ ounce) cream of
   mushroom soup

1 jar (8 ounce) picante sauce
Corn chips

Brown beef and sausage. Drain well. Melt cheese in a saucepan. Add beef, sausage, soup and picante sauce. Mix well. Serve warm with corn chips.

SERVES 20

This is an old fashioned crowd pleaser! Not exactly elegant, but great for large informal parties.

CAROL MITCHELL (MRS. BRUCE)
MOTHER OF LISA MITCHELL PARRISH AND JEAN MITCHELL SALISBURY, FORMER HIES STUDENTS

TAILGATE CORN DIP

1 package (10 ounce) frozen
   shoepeg corn, thawed
1 package (8 ounce) cream cheese,
   softened

1 stick margarine
Chopped jalapeños to taste
Salt to taste

1 tablespoon garlic powder
Large scoop corn chips

Combine corn, cream cheese and butter in a baking dish. Add jalapeños, salt and garlic powder. Bake at 350 degrees 45 minutes. Stir occasionally until cream cheese and butter melts. Serve with scoop corn chips.

SERVES 8

TARRAGON-CHIVE DEVILED EGGS

1 dozen hard-cooked eggs, peeled
  and separated
½ cup mayonnaise

1 tablespoon lemon juice
¼ teaspoon Tabasco sauce
2 tablespoons chopped chives

2 tablespoons chopped tarragon
½ tablespoon dry mustard

Combine egg yolks, mayonnaise, lemon juice, Tabasco, chives, tarragon and mustard. Mix well. Pipe mixture into egg whites. Refrigerate.

SERVES 12

WARMED CRANBERRY BRIE

⅓ cup crushed cranberry sauce
2 tablespoons brown sugar
¼ teaspoon brandy

⅛ teaspoon ground nutmeg
1 wheel (8 ounce) Brie cheese

2 tablespoons chopped pecans
Sliced apples and crackers

Combine cranberry sauce, brown sugar, brandy and nutmeg. Remove top rind of Brie cheese. Spoon cranberry mixture over top of Brie cheese. Sprinkle with pecans. Bake at 500 degrees 4-5 minutes. Let stand until set. Serve with apple slices and crackers.

SERVES 8-10

WILD MUSHROOM CROSTINI

36 (⅓ inch) baguette slices
2 tablespoons olive oil
⅓ cup chopped shallots
2¼ cups chopped oyster mushrooms
2¼ cups chopped stemmed shiitake
　mushrooms

1¼ cups chopped chanterelle
　mushrooms
1 garlic clove, minced
¼ cup whipping cream
1 teaspoon minced rosemary

½ teaspoon lemon zest
Salt and pepper to taste
1 cup grated Fontina cheese
½ cup grated Parmesan cheese

Arrange baguette slices on rimmed baking sheet. Toast at 375 degrees 9 minutes until golden browned. Cool. (May prepare 2 days in advance. Store in airtight container at room temperature.)

Heat oil in large skillet. Sauté shallots 1 minute. Add all mushrooms. Sauté 6 minutes until beginning to brown. Stir in garlic and sauté 1 minute. Remove from heat. Stir in cream, rosemary and lemon zest. Add salt and pepper. Cool. Stir in Fontina cheese and Parmesan cheese. (May prepare 2 days in advance. Cover and refrigerate.)

Top each toast slice with about 1 tablespoon mushroom topping. Place on rimmed baking sheet. Working in batches, broil 3 minutes until cheese melts and is lightly browned. Watch closely. Transfer to serving platter and serve warm.

SERVES 10-12

CHAMPAGNE PUNCH

1 can (20 ounce) crushed pineapple
  in heavy syrup
1 cup lemon juice

1 cup maraschino cherry juice
1 cup dark rum
½ cup brandy

1 bottle inexpensive brut
  champagne, chilled

Combine pineapple, lemon juice, cherry juice, rum and brandy in a punch bowl or pitcher. Mix well. Refrigerate 30 minutes. Add champagne just before serving.

SERVES 8-10

I found the recipe this past summer and used it all summer long for company. Be careful, it is delicious, but very potent. Serve with a brunch menu or as cocktails at the beach.

 CREAMY DATE NUT SHAKE

2 frozen bananas
1½ cups rice milk or soy milk

1 tablespoon cashews, almonds or
  pecans

5 pitted dates

Peel bananas, break in half and place in zip-top freezer bag. Lay flat and freeze overnight. Combine milk and cashews in a blender. Blend 1 minute. Add dates and blend 30 seconds. Break frozen bananas into small pieces and add to blender. Blend 30 seconds. If too thick add milk and if too thin add more bananas.

SERVES 2-3

DARK N' STORMY COCKTAILS

1½ ounces Gosling's Black Seal rum   Good quality ginger beer   Lime wedges for garnish

Pour rum into a glass with cracked ice. Fill to top with ginger beer. Top with lime wedge.

SERVES 1

 # FRUIT SMOOTHIE

1 cup orange juice   8 frozen peach slices   1 cup ice
1 cup cranberry juice   6 frozen strawberries

Combine orange juice, cranberry juice, peaches and strawberries into a blender. Process until smooth. Add ice and blend to desired consistency. Serve immediately.

SERVES 4 (8 OUNCE) PORTIONS

SPICE TEA/FRIENDSHIP TEA

2 cups orange flavored powdered   1¼ cups powdered lemonade drink   1 cup sugar
   drink mix   mix   ½ cup instant tea mix
                                    1 teaspoon cinnamon   1 teaspoon ground cloves

Combine orange mix, lemonade mix, cinnamon, sugar, instant tea and cloves. Mix well. Pour mixture into a jar or container with airtight seal. To serve, add 1-2 teaspoons tea mixture to 1 cup hot water and stir.

SERVES 1

HUNTSVILLE "PARTY" ICED TEA

1 quart water	10 tablespoons bottled lemon juice	2 cups sugar
12 tea bags	4 oranges, juiced	Lemon wedges or mint leaves for garnish

Boil water and add tea bags. Steep 5 minutes. Add lemon juice, orange juice and sugar. Mix well. Add enough cold water to equal 2 quarts tea. Garnish with lemon wedges or mint leaves. May store tea for 2 days.

SERVES 8-10

This tea was always served at ladies lunches and parties growing up in Huntsville. It became know as "party" tea.

MOJITO

1½ ounces light rum	1 lime wedge	Lemon-lime carbonated beverage
4-5 mint sprigs	½ ounce lime juice	

Muddle together rum, mint, lime wedge and lime juice. Cover with ice and shake well. Strain into a highball glass. Pour in carbonated beverage. Garnish with a mint sprig.

SERVES 1

PIMM'S COCKTAIL

2 lime wedges	2 orange slices	Ginger ale
8 mint sprigs	2 ounces Pimm's No.1	Cucumber slice for garnish

Place lime wedges, mint and orange slices into a cocktail shaker. Lightly muddle to bruise citrus skins. Leave skin on fruits to release fragrant and flavorful oils. Add ice and Pimm's. Shake gently. Strain into rock glass. Top off with ginger ale. Garnish with cucumber slice.

SERVES 1

SUMMER SANGRÍA

½ cup sugar
½ cup lemon juice
4 cups cold dry white wine

½ cup orange juice
¼ cup triple sec
10 ounces cold club soda

Lemon slices, strawberries, orange slices, or mint for garnish

Combine sugar, lemon juice, wine, orange juice and triple sec. Mix well. Refrigerate until ready to serve. Add club soda and garnish before serving.

SERVES 4-6

WHITE SANGRÍA

1 bottle (750 ml) white wine
¼ cup triple sec
¼ cup sugar

1 lemon, thinly sliced
1 cup frozen peaches, thawed

1 cup frozen raspberries, thawed
2 cups club soda

Combine wine, triple sec, sugar, lemon slices, peaches and raspberries in a large pitcher. Stir until sugar dissolves. Cover tightly with plastic wrap. Refrigerate 2 hours. Before serving, stir in club soda and pour over ice.

SERVES 8

Use an inexpensive dry white wine like Pinot Grigio or Vino Verde. May also substitute lemon lime carbonated beverage for club soda for sweeter sangría.

 BREADS AND
BREAKFAST

Aunt Ruth's Hen and Cornbread Dressing

1 hen
Salt to taste
1 prepared skillet cornbread,
    made with 6 eggs

4 baked biscuits
4 slices wheat or white bread
½ sleeve saltine crackers
1 onion, chopped

2 stalks celery, finely chopped
½ teaspoon rubbed sage
Pepper to taste

Cook hen in salted boiling water. Remove and cool hen, reserving broth. Remove meat from bone. Crumble cornbread, biscuits, bread and crackers in a bowl. Add onions, celery, sage and pepper. Place meat on bottom of 2 quart casserole dish. Top with bread mixture, covering all meat. Pour on reserved broth until bread is moist. Bake at 350 degrees 30 minutes. Broil until top is browned.

SERVES 8-10

This is truly a crowd pleaser and is always the first thing to go.

Banana Muffins

1 stick butter, softened
1 cup packed brown sugar
3 ripe bananas, mashed

1 egg, beaten
¼ cup sour cream
1½ cups all-purpose flour

1 teaspoon baking soda
1 teaspoon baking powder

Beat butter and sugar until smooth. Blend in bananas, egg and sour cream. In a separate bowl, combine flour, baking soda and baking powder. Add to banana mixture. Stir until just moistened. Pour batter into greased muffin tins or greased 9 x 5-inch loaf pan. Bake at 325 degrees 45 minutes or until golden browned and tester comes out clean. Cool on wire rack.

SERVES 8-10

"CAT-HEAD" BISCUITS

3½ cups wheat flour or half cake
   flour and half all-purpose flour
1 tablespoon baking powder

1 teaspoon salt
1¼ sticks unsalted butter, cubed and
   chilled

1¼-1½ cups buttermilk, room
   temperature

Combine flour, baking powder and salt. Mix well with a whisk. Cut in butter with two knives or pastry blender until uniformly mixed and no lumps. Stir in 1¼ cups buttermilk just until blended. Do not over mix. Add more buttermilk or flour as needed.

Turn dough out onto a lightly floured surface. Using floured fingers, lightly pat dough together. With a floured rolling pin, roll dough to ¾ inch thickness. Cut dough with a floured 2½ inch biscuit cutter. Quickly punch out biscuits, do not twist cutter in dough. Avoid touching dough with hands. Gather up scraps and cut out more biscuits. Place biscuits close but not touching on an ungreased baking sheet. Bake at 450 degrees 15-18 minutes or until lightly browned.

SERVES 6

May double recipe easily.

SARAH WARREN'S BISCUITS

1 cup self-rising flour

1 stick butter, softened

1 container (8 ounce) sour cream

Combine flour, butter and sour cream. Mix well. Spoon batter into two greased mini-muffin pans. Bake at 400 degrees 12-15 minutes or until golden browned.

SERVES 24 MINI BISCUITS

BREAD RING

1 stick butter	3 packages (8 ounces each) refrigerated crescent rolls

Melt butter in Bundt pan in oven. Remove rolls from package and do not unfold. Lay three rolls, end to end, around the bottom of pan, squeezing rolls into one layer. Bake at 375 degrees about 45 minutes or until browned. (Top will be fairly dark brown.) Cool in pan 5 minutes. Invert onto a serving dish. Cut into 20 slices.

SERVES 8-10

CHOCOLATE CHIP BANANA BREAD

⅔ cup sugar

2 eggs, beaten

2 medium ripe bananas, mashed

½ cup vegetable oil or applesauce

1¾ cups all-purpose flour

1 teaspoon baking soda

½ teaspoon baking powder

1½ teaspoons pumpkin pie spice

1 teaspoon cinnamon

1 cup mini semi-sweet chocolate chips

1 cup chopped walnuts

½ teaspoon vanilla

Beat together sugar, eggs and bananas. Stir in oil. Combine flour, baking soda, baking powder, pumpkin spice and cinnamon. Gradually add flour mixture to creamed mixture. Stir in chocolate chips, walnuts and vanilla. Mix well. Divide batter among four greased 5 x 3-inch loaf pans. Bake at 350 degrees 45-50 minutes or until tester comes out clean.

SERVES 12

KIRK AND LIZZIE DUNCAN
CURRENT HEADMASTER

Our favorite way to eat this is a big, hot slice in a bowl with half-and-half poured on top.

CREAM SCONES WITH CURRENTS
"THE ONLY SCONES YOU WILL EVER EAT"

2 cups all-purpose flour
3 tablespoons sugar
1 tablespoon baking powder

½ teaspoon salt
5 tablespoons unsalted butter, cut into ¼ inch cubes and chilled

½ cup currents
1 cup heavy cream

Pulse flour, sugar, baking powder and salt in a food processor 6 times. Scatter butter over top. Pulse about 12 times until mixture resembles coarse meal with a few large lumps. Add currents and quickly pulse to combine. Transfer dough to a large bowl. Stir in cream until a dough forms.

Turn dough onto a floured surface and knead into a slightly sticky ball. Press dough into a 9 inch round cake pan. Flip molded dough onto a cutting board. Cut into 8 wedges. Place on ungreased baking sheet. Bake at 450 degrees 12-15 minutes or until lightly browned. Cool on wire rack at least 10 minutes.

SERVES 8

Ginger Scones-substitute ½ cup chopped crystallized ginger for currents.

Cranberry Orange Scones-add 1 teaspoon orange zest with butter and substitute ¾ cup dried cranberries for currents.

CHRISTMAS MORNING MONKEY BREAD

1 cup sugar
¼ cup packed brown sugar

1 tablespoon cinnamon
3 packages (12 ounces each)
    refrigerated biscuits

1 stick butter, melted

Combine sugar, brown sugar and cinnamon. Cut biscuits into fourths. Add to sugar mixture and toss to coat. Place biscuits in a greased Bundt pan. Pour excess sugar mixture on top. Pour butter evenly over biscuits. Bake at 350 degrees 25-30 minutes. May prepare biscuits with sugar mixture and refrigerate overnight. Pour butter on next morning before baking.

SERVES 12

May substitute Splenda for sugar for healthier biscuits.

GINGERBREAD

1 stick butter, softened
½ cup sugar
2 egg yolks
½ cup molasses

½ cup buttermilk
1¼ cups all-purpose flour
1 teaspoon baking powder
1 teaspoon ground ginger

½ teaspoon cinnamon
¼ teaspoon ground cloves
½ teaspoon baking soda
2 eggs whites, slightly beaten

Cream butter, sugar, egg yolks, molasses and buttermilk. Combine flour, baking powder, ginger, cinnamon and cloves. Stir baking soda into creamed mixture. Add flour mixture and egg whites. Pour batter into a 9 x 5-inch loaf pan. Bake at 350 degrees 30-40 minutes.

SERVES 8-10

GRANDMOTHER'S FAMOUS CRANBERRY BREAD

2 cups all-purpose flour
1 cup sugar
1½ teaspoons baking powder
1 teaspoon salt

½ teaspoon baking soda
4 tablespoons butter, softened
1 egg, beaten
1 teaspoon orange zest

¾ cup orange juice
1½ cups golden raisins
1½ cups fresh or frozen cranberries, chopped

Sift together flour, sugar, baking powder, salt and baking soda. Cut in butter until crumbly. Add egg, orange zest and orange juice all at once. Stir just until moistened. Fold in raisins and cranberries. Spoon batter into a greased 9 x 5-inch loaf pan. Bake at 350 degrees 1 hour, 10 minutes or until tester comes out clean. Remove from pan. Cool on wire rack.

SERVES 8-10

May substitute cranberries for raisins to have all cranberry.

When my daughter was in preschool, she belonged to a "Book Club" and received a new book each month by mail. The November selection was Cranberry Thanksgiving by Wende and Harry Devlin. This recipe was printed at the end of the book and we made it many times.

SAUSAGE MUFFINS

½ pound hot sausage
⅓ cup chopped green onions
1 package (6 ounce) biscuit mix

½ teaspoon dry mustard
¼ teaspoon cayenne pepper

½ cup milk
¾ cup shredded Cheddar cheese

Brown sausage and green onions. Drain well. Add biscuit mix, mustard, cayenne, milk and Cheddar cheese. Spoon batter into mini-muffin pans. Bake at 400 degrees 10-12 minutes or until golden browned.

SERVES 24 MINI-MUFFINS

Yorkshire Pudding

6 tablespoons all-purpose flour
2 tablespoons cold water

2 eggs
Milk

Roast drippings

Combine flour and water. Beat in eggs, one at a time. Add milk until consistency of cream. Let stand. Place a small amount of roast drippings into muffin pans. Heat in a 450 degree oven. When fat smokes, remove pan. Spoon batter into individual cups. Bake 15-20 minutes.

SERVES 4-6

Strawberry Bread

3 cups all-purpose flour
1 teaspoon salt
2 cups sugar

1 teaspoon baking soda
1 tablespoon cinnamon
4 eggs, beaten

2 cups frozen strawberries, thawed
1¼ cups vegetable oil
1¼ cups chopped pecans

Combine flour, salt, sugar, baking soda and cinnamon. Add eggs, strawberries, oil and pecans. Stir until just moistened. Spoon batter into two well greased 9 x 5-inch loaf pans. Bake at 350 degrees 60-70 minutes or until tester comes out clean. Cool in pan 5 minutes. Remove to wire rack to cool. Freezes well.

SERVES 16

STARTER SOURDOUGH BREAD

STARTER

¾ cup sugar

3 tablespoons potato flakes

1 cup warm water

1 package active dry yeast

FEEDING STARTER

¾ cup sugar

3 tablespoons instant potato flakes

1 cup warm water

BREAD

1 tablespoon salt

1 tablespoon sugar

½ cup vegetable oil

1½ cups warm water

6 cups bread flour

STARTER

Combine sugar, potato flakes, water and yeast. Cover 1 day. Stir in pour into a quart jar, leaving air spaces in lid. Refrigerate at least 2 days before feeding to use in making bread.

FEEDING STARTER

Mix sugar, potato flakes and water into starter. Let stand at room temperature 8-12 hours. Remove 1 cup mixture to make bread. Refrigerate remaining starter for next batch. Feed every 3-5 days.

BREAD

Combine 1 cup starter with salt, sugar, oil, water and flour. Turn dough into a large greased bowl so oil is on top. Cover lightly. Let stand overnight or throughout the day. Divide dough into three portions. Place in three greased 9 x 5-inch loaf pans. Let rise overnight or throughout the day. Bake at 350 degrees 50 minutes.

SERVES 3 LOAVES

Be sure to hang around while bread is baking because the smell is wonderful.

BREAKFAST CAKE

½ cup chopped nuts
1 package (11 ounce) frozen yeast rolls

1 package (3 ounce) butterscotch pudding mix, not instant
1 stick butter

½ teaspoon cinnamon
¾ cup packed brown sugar

Grease and flour Bundt pan. Place nuts in bottom of pan. Place frozen yeast rolls over nuts. Sprinkle pudding mix over rolls. Combine butter, cinnamon and brown sugar. Sprinkle over rolls. Cover with a towel. Let stand overnight. Bake at 350 degrees 25-30 minutes.

SERVES 10-12

This is great to serve overnight guests for breakfast or just something special for your family.

BREAKFAST CASSEROLE

6 slices buttered bread, crust removed
1 pound pork sausage, browned

1½ cups grated Cheddar or Swiss cheese

6 eggs, beaten
2 cups half-and-half

Place bread in a greased 13 x 9 x 2-inch baking dish. Spoon crumbled sausage over bread. Sprinkle with Cheddar cheese. Whisk together eggs and half-and-half. Mix well. Pour egg mixture over cheese. Cover and refrigerate overnight. Bake, uncovered, at 350 degrees 45 minutes.

SERVES 8-10

CHEESE BLINTZES

2 egg yolks
½ cup sugar
2 packages (8 ounces each) cream
    cheese, softened

2 large loaves square white
    sandwich bread
1 tablespoon cinnamon

½ cup sugar
2 sticks butter, melted

Combine egg yolks, sugar and cream cheese until smooth. Cut crusts off bread. Gently flatten bread with a rolling pin. Spread cream cheese mixture over bread to all the corners. Combine cinnamon and sugar. Roll up bread and dip in butter. Dredge rolls in sugar mixture. Place seam side down on a baking sheet. Freeze at least 2 hours. Bake at 350 degrees 15-20 minutes.

SERVES 52 BLINTZES

CHRISTMAS BREAKFAST CASSEROLE

2 packages (8 ounces each)
    refrigerated crescent rolls
1 pound ground sausage

7 eggs
1 package (8 ounce) shredded sharp
    Cheddar cheese

3 tablespoons butter

Press one package rolls into bottom of greased 13 x 9 x 2-inch baking dish, sealing all perforations. Brown sausage. Remove from heat. Add eggs and Cheddar cheese. Mix well. Pour mixture over dough. Place second package rolls on top, sealing all perforations. Dot with butter. Bake at 350 degrees 30 minutes or until golden browned.

SERVES 6-8

May also add chopped green onions and mushrooms. May prepare a day in advance and refrigerate overnight.

CHEESE EGG GRITS

2 cups quick yellow grits
8 cups water
Salt to taste
2 sticks butter

1 roll (6 ounce) garlic cheese roll
2 eggs, beaten
1½ cups milk
Cayenne pepper to taste

1 package (8 ounce) shredded sharp
Cheddar cheese
Paprika for garnish

Combine grits, water and salt in a saucepan. Cook until thickened. Remove from heat. Stir in butter, garlic cheese, eggs, milk and cayenne until smooth. Pour mixture into a buttered casserole dish. Sprinkle with Cheddar cheese and paprika. Bake at 350 degrees 1 hour. Cool 20 minutes until set.

SERVES 8-10

CHEESE GRITS

1 quart milk
1 teaspoon salt
⅛ teaspoon white pepper

1 stick butter
1 cup quick grits
5⅓ tablespoons butter, melted

⅓ cup grated Parmesan cheese
1 cup grated Swiss or Gruyère
cheese

Heat milk, salt, pepper and butter just until boiling. Stir in grits. Cook, stirring constantly until thickened. Remove from heat. Beat 5 minutes. Pour grits into a casserole dish. Pour butter on top. Sprinkle with Parmesan and Swiss cheese. Bake at 400 degrees 25-30 minutes.

SERVES 8

One and half recipes will fit into a 3 quart glass dish.

ORIGINAL PANCAKE HOUSE GERMAN PANCAKE

3 large eggs
¾ cup milk
½ teaspoon vanilla

¾ cup all-purpose flour
½ teaspoon salt
1½ teaspoons butter

Powdered sugar to taste
Lemon wedges, butter or syrup to taste

Whisk together eggs, milk, vanilla, flour and salt until very smooth. Melt butter in a 12 inch cast iron skillet. Pour batter into hot skillet. Place skillet into oven. Bake at 450 degrees 15 minutes. Reduce heat to 350 degrees and bake an additional 10 minutes.

Remove from oven. Sprinkle with powdered sugar. Squeeze lemon wedges over pancake or top with butter and syrup. Roll up pancake like a burrito.

SERVES 6

SAUSAGE GRITS SOUTHERN CASSEROLE

1 pound sausage
3 cups cooked grits

2½ cups shredded sharp Cheddar cheese
1 teaspoon butter

1½ cups milk
3 eggs, beaten

Brown and crumble sausage. Drain well. Spoon sausage into a lightly greased 13 x 9 x 2-inch baking dish. Combine cooked grits, Cheddar cheese and butter. Whisk together milk and eggs. Add to grits mixture. Pour mixture over sausage. Bake at 350 degrees 1 hour.

SERVES 8-10

COUNTRY BREAKFAST STRATA
WITH SAUSAGE, FONTINA AND ROSEMARY

8 ounces turkey sausage, casing removed

1 medium onion, chopped

1 tablespoon extra virgin olive oil

½ loaf hearty country or egg bread, 1-2 days old, cut into ½ inch slices

1 tablespoon chopped rosemary

2 cups heavy cream

½ cup half-and-half

8 eggs

½ teaspoon salt

1 teaspoon pepper

2 tomatoes, cut into ¼ inch slices

3 cups grated Fontina or Swiss cheese

Brown sausage and onions in oil about 10-12 minutes, breaking up sausage. Remove from heat. If using fresh bread, lightly toast bread. Whisk together rosemary, cream, half-and-half, eggs, salt and pepper. Arrange half bread in bottom of a buttered 13 x 9 x 2-inch baking dish. Top with half sausage mixture, tomatoes and Fontina cheese. Repeat layers of bread, sausage, tomatoes and cheese. Pour egg mixture over all. Cover and refrigerate 8 hours or overnight. Place baking dish on baking sheet. Bake, uncovered, at 350 degrees 45 minutes or until golden browned. Cool 10 minutes.

SERVES 8-10

SALADS

BABY ARUGULA WITH SMITHFIELD HAM, MAYTAG BLUE CHEESE AND FRESH FIG VINAIGRETTE

2 tablespoons butter
2 cups chopped figs
¾ cup sugar
Salt and pepper to taste
¾ cup cider vinegar

2 cups vegetable oil
4 (½ inch thick) slices brioche
¼ cup olive oil
8 cups arugula, rinsed and picked
4 figs, quartered

4 ounces Smithfield ham, julienned and fried until crispy
6 ounces crumbled Maytag blue cheese
Cracked black pepper to taste for garnish

Preheat oven to 400 degrees. Brown butter with 1½ cups chopped figs and sugar. Add salt and pepper. Remove from heat. Transfer to a food processor. Purée for 1 minute. Add vinegar and process 30 seconds. With machine running, slowly add vegetable oil until dressing is emulsified. Add salt and pepper. Fold in reserved ½ cup figs. Pour dressing into a saucepan and keep warm.

Remove crust from brioche and cut into ½ inch cubes. Toss bread cubes with olive oil. Sprinkle with salt and pepper. Place cubes on a baking sheet. Bake about 8-10 minutes until golden browned. Remove and cool.

Toss arugula with desired amount of dressing. Mound arugula in center of individual plates. Arrange quartered figs, ham and croutons around arugula. Crumble blue cheese on top. Garnish with pepper around rim of plate.

SERVES 4

BROCCOLI SALAD

1 cup mayonnaise	3 packages broccoli pieces	½ red onion, chopped
2 tablespoons sugar	½ cup raisins	8 slices bacon, cooked and crumbled
1½ tablespoons red wine vinegar		

Blend mayonnaise, sugar and vinegar until smooth. In a salad bowl, combine broccoli pieces, raisins and red onions. Pour on dressing and toss to coat. Refrigerate and marinate 2-3 hours. Add crumbled bacon just before serving.

SERVES 12

May also use 3 packages of prewashed, precut broccoli pieces.

BREAD MARKET POTATO SALAD

5 pounds red potatoes	½ cup chopped parsley	1 teaspoon pepper
1 tablespoon kosher salt	1⅓ cups chopped yellow onions	2 cups salad dressing
1 tablespoon white vinegar	1 teaspoon celery salt	

Cover potatoes in cold water in a large stockpot. Add salt and bring to boil. Reduce heat and cook 30 minutes until tender. Drain well. Cut potatoes into quarters while warm.

In a separate bowl, whisk together vinegar, parsley, onions, celery salt, pepper and salad dressing. Mix well. Combine dressing and potatoes. Refrigerate until ready to serve.

SERVES 12

BREAD MARKET TUNA SALAD

2 cans (6 ounces each) tuna in water
¼ cup finely chopped celery

1 green onion, finely chopped
¼ cup grated carrots

⅛ teaspoon pepper
¼ cup mayonnaise

Drain tuna well. Flake into a bowl. Add celery, green onions, carrots and pepper. Stir in mayonnaise. May prepare ahead and add mayonnaise just before serving.

SERVES 4

CHICKEN SALAD WITH GRAPES AND NUTS

3 pounds boneless skinless chicken
  breast halves
1 cup mayonnaise

½ cup plus 2 tablespoons sour
  cream
2 tablespoons lemon juice
1 teaspoon pepper

⅔ cup chopped celery
1¼ cups red seedless grapes,
  quartered
¾ cup walnuts, chopped

Cover chicken with water. Bring to boil. Cook 30 minutes or until chicken is cooked through. Cool and chop.

Combine mayonnaise, sour cream, lemon juice and pepper. Mix well. Combine chicken, mayonnaise mixture, celery, grapes and nuts. Mix well. Refrigerate until ready to serve.

SERVES 6

Cut grapes in half after measured in cup. May add salt to taste. May also substitute toasted almonds for walnuts.

CHINESE NOODLE SALAD

DRESSING

1 cup vegetable oil

½ cup sugar

½ cup rice vinegar

2 tablespoons soy sauce

SALAD

2 packages (3 ounces each) Ramen noodles, no seasoning packet

1 stick margarine

1 package (2½ ounce) slivered almonds

1 medium head Napa cabbage, chopped

6 green onions, diced

½ cup toasted sunflower seeds

DRESSING

Combine oil, sugar, vinegar and soy sauce in a jar or bottle. Shake well. Let stand 20 minutes while sugar dissolves and dressing slightly thickens.

SALAD

Break noodles in small pieces. Melt margarine in a skillet. Sauté noodles and almonds, stirring occasionally, until golden browned. Drain on paper towels. Cool to room temperature. About 20 minutes before serving, place cabbage in a large serving bowl. Add noodles, almonds, green onions and sunflower seeds. Shake dressing and pour over salad. Toss to coat. Refrigerate until ready to serve.

SERVES 4

CHUTNEY CHICKEN SALAD

1 cup mayonnaise

½ cup Major Grey chutney

8 boneless skinless chicken breast
halves, cooked and cubed

2 stalks celery, chopped

4 green apples, peeled, chopped and
sprinkled with lemon juice

4 green onions, chopped

½ cup red seedless grapes, halved

½ cup pecans, chopped and toasted

2 cups brown rice, cooked

Whisk together mayonnaise and chutney. Add chicken, celery, apples, green onions, grapes, pecans and rice. Refrigerate until ready to serve.

SERVES 12-15

CURRY CHICKEN SALAD

3 pounds boneless skinless chicken
breast halves

1½ cups mayonnaise

1¾ teaspoons lemon juice

1¼ tablespoons Dijon mustard

2 garlic cloves, crushed

2 teaspoons curry powder

1¾ teaspoons ground ginger

⅔ cup almonds, sliced

½ cup golden seedless raisins

Cover chicken with water in a stockpot. Bring to boil. Cook 30 minutes or until cooked through. Cool and chop.

Combine mayonnaise, lemon juice, mustard, garlic, curry and ginger. Mix well. Combine chicken, mayonnaise mixture, almonds and raisins. Mix well. Refrigerate until ready to serve.

SERVES 6

May use grilled or baked chicken. If on a tight schedule, purchase a cooked chicken.

GREEK PASTA SALAD

1 pound bowtie pasta
1 cup chopped black olives
1 cup chopped artichoke hearts
4 tomatoes, chopped

¾ cup feta cheese, crumbled
3 green onions, chopped
½ cup chopped red onions
1½ teaspoons kosher salt

½ teaspoon pepper
½ cup basil purée, p. 76
½ cup Greek salad dressing

Cook pasta until al dente. Plunge into cold water and drain. Combine olives, artichokes, tomatoes, feta cheese, green onions, red onions, salt and pepper in a large bowl. Add pasta. Stir in basil purée and Greek dressing. Toss to coat.

SERVES 12

Pasta should always be measured uncooked unless specified. May substitute prepared basil pesto for basil purée and balsamic vinaigrette for Greek dressing.

 # GREEK SALAD

½ cup extra virgin olive oil
3 tablespoons red wine vinegar
3 tablespoons lemon juice
2 tablespoons chopped oregano
1 tablespoon chopped mint

Salt and pepper to taste
4 romaine hearts, torn
6 medium tomatoes, cored and cut
   into wedges

6 Kirby cucumbers, peeled and cut
   into ½ inch slices
1½ cups crumbled feta cheese
1 cup Gaeta olives, pitted

Whisk together oil, vinegar, lemon juice, oregano, mint, salt and pepper. In a separate large bowl, combine romaine, tomatoes, cucumbers, feta cheese and olives. Pour on dressing and toss to coat. Serve immediately.

SERVES 12

❤ INSALATA D'INVERNO
(WINTER SALAD)

4 large oranges
1 small red onion, halved and thinly sliced

Kosher salt and pepper to taste
Extra-virgin olive oil to taste

¼ cup oil-cured black olives, whole or thinly sliced

Peel oranges with a sharp knife, removing white pith. Cut in half lengthwise and in half crosswise. Cut sections into ¼ inch slices. Place in a bowl and set aside.

Sprinkle onions with salt. Let stand 10 minutes. Just prior to serving, sprinkle pepper and drizzle oil over oranges and onions in separate bowls. Arrange oranges on a serving plate. Top with onions and garnish with olives.

SERVES 4

LARK AND DOVE CAESAR SALAD

1 medium garlic clove, well minced
1 anchovy, well minced
1 tablespoon grated Parmesan cheese
1 tablespoon Worcestershire sauce
¼ teaspoon dry mustard

Dash of Tabasco sauce
1 egg yolk
½ lemon, juiced
3 tablespoons vegetable oil
1 tablespoon red wine vinegar

2 cups romaine lettuce, rinsed and dried
2 tablespoons grated Parmesan cheese
½ cup croutons
Pepper to taste

Whisk together garlic and anchovy. Add Parmesan cheese, Worcestershire sauce, mustard and Tabasco. Mix well. Blend in egg yolk and lemon juice. Whisk in oil and vinegar. Place romaine in a bowl. Pour on dressing and gently toss to coat. Add Parmesan cheese and croutons and toss. Top with more Parmesan cheese and pepper.

SERVES 2

I remember having this wonderful salad prepared at the table. It was the best Caesar salad I have ever had.

HEARTS OF PALM SALAD

DRESSING

¼ small onion, chopped

3 tablespoons apple cider vinegar

2 teaspoons spicy brown mustard

½ teaspoon sugar

½ teaspoon salt

¼ teaspoon pepper

1 cup olive oil

SALAD

12-16 slices bacon, cooked
crisp and crumbled

1 jar (7 ounce) hearts of palm,
chopped

1 jar (8 ounce) artichoke hearts,
chopped

Romaine lettuce, torn

4 ounces blue cheese

DRESSING

Combine onions and vinegar in a blender. Process until onions are puréed. Add mustard, sugar, salt and pepper. Process until well blended. Slowly add oil, processing at high speed until thickened.

SALAD

Combine bacon, hearts of palm, artichokes, romaine and blue cheese. Pour on dressing and toss to coat.

SERVES 4-6

May add chopped fried chicken strips.

LAYERED SALAD

1 head iceberg lettuce, torn into
    bite size pieces
1 cup chopped celery
1 cup chopped bell pepper

1 cup chopped yellow or red onions
1 package (10 ounce) frozen green
    peas, thawed
1 cup mayonnaise

1 tablespoon sugar
1-2 cups shredded Cheddar cheese
10 slices bacon, cooked and
    crumbled

Arrange lettuce in bottom of a round salad bowl. Layer in order celery, peppers, onions and peas. Carefully spread mayonnaise on top. Sprinkle with sugar. Cover tightly with plastic wrap. Refrigerate overnight. Before serving, layer Cheddar cheese and bacon.

SERVES 12

MIXED GREENS AND STRAWBERRY SALAD

1 tablespoon sherry or raspberry
    vinegar
1 teaspoon minced green onion or
    shallot
1 teaspoon honey or maple syrup
Kosher salt and freshly ground
    pepper to taste

2½ tablespoons hazelnut oil
4 cups arugula, washed and spun
    dry, discarding tough stems
4 cups mixed greens, washed and
    spun dry

1½ cups strawberries, washed,
    hulled and quartered
½ cup toasted hazelnuts, coarsely
    chopped
½ cup goat cheese, crumbled

Whisk together vinegar, green onions, honey, salt and pepper in a small non-reactive bowl. Slowly whisk in oil until blended. Combine arugula, greens and strawberries in a large serving bowl. Drizzle with dressing and toss to coat. Divide salad among individual plates. Top with nuts and goat cheese.

SERVES 4-6

LAYERED SOUTHWESTERN SALAD

DRESSING

⅓ cup chopped cilantro

½ cup lime juice

½ cup olive oil

½ cup sour cream

1 teaspoon sugar

½ teaspoon salt

½ teaspoon pepper

SALAD

1 head red leaf or romaine lettuce

5 plum tomatoes, sliced

1 can (15 ounce) black beans, rinsed

1 small red onion, chopped

1 package (8 ounce) shredded
  Mexican four cheese blend

1 can (15 ounce) whole kernel corn
  with red peppers

1 can (6 ounce) sliced black olives

2 cups crushed tortilla chips

DRESSING

Combine cilantro, lime juice, oil, sour cream, sugar, salt and pepper in a food processor. Blend until smooth. Refrigerate.

SALAD

Layer in order in a 13 x 9 x 2-inch baking dish, the lettuce, tomatoes, black beans, onions, Mexican cheese, corn, black olives and tortilla crumbs. Pour dressing evenly over top.

SERVES 10-12

MIXED GREENS AND GOAT CHEESE

DRESSING

¼ cup olive oil

2 garlic cloves, peeled and halved

1 tablespoon chopped basil

2 tablespoons red wine vinegar

2 tablespoons Dijon mustard

Salt and pepper to taste

SALAD

1 cup breadcrumbs

1 tablespoon chopped thyme

1 tablespoon chopped parsley

1 tablespoon chopped basil

Salt and pepper to taste

3 logs (4 ounces each) goat cheese

2 egg whites

1 tablespoon olive oil

1 package (10 ounce) baby mixed
greens

DRESSING

Combine oil and garlic in a small bowl and cover with plastic wrap. Microwave 30 seconds. Remove garlic and mash with a fork. Combine garlic, basil, vinegar and mustard until smooth. Gradually whisk in reserved olive oil. Sprinkle with salt and pepper. Prepare at least 1-8 hours or up to a day in advance.

SALAD

Combine breadcrumbs, thyme, parsley, basil, salt and pepper. Cut goat cheese in half lengthwise and flatten to ½ inch. Dip goat cheese in egg white and dredge in breadcrumb mixture. Cover with plastic wrap and refrigerate 1-8 hours. Cook goat cheese in oil about 3 minutes per side until golden browned. Toss greens with dressing and top with warm goat cheese.

SERVES 4-6

ROQUEFORT PEAR SALAD

¼ cup sugar
½ cup pecans
⅓ cup olive oil
3 tablespoons red wine vinegar
1½ teaspoons sugar

1½ teaspoons Dijon mustard
1 garlic clove, chopped
½ teaspoon salt
Pepper to taste
1 head lettuce, torn

3 pears, peeled, cored and chopped
5 ounces blue cheese, crumbled
1 avocado, peeled, pitted and sliced
½ cup thinly sliced green onions

Heat sugar and pecans in a skillet over medium heat. Cook and stir until sugar melts and pecans are caramelized. Transfer to wax paper. Cool and chop.

Blend oil, vinegar, sugar, mustard, garlic, salt and pepper until smooth. Layer lettuce, pears, blue cheese, avocados and green onions in a large serving bowl. Pour dressing over salad. Sprinkle with pecans.

SERVES 4-6

ORZO SALAD

1 package (8 ounce) orzo pasta, cooked al dente, drained and refrigerated

1 cup sun-dried tomatoes in oil, chopped
½ cup toasted slivered almonds
3 green onions, chopped

⅓ pound chopped spinach
Greek and Three cheese dressing
Parmesan cheese and feta cheese to taste

Combine orzo, tomatoes, almonds, green onions and spinach. Pour on a small combination of Greek and Three cheese dressing. Top with Parmesan cheese and feta cheese. Best if prepared a day in advance.

SERVES 6-8

POTATO SALAD

4 pounds small new red potatoes
2 tablespoons lemon juice

1 tablespoon dried dill or
   2 tablespoons chopped fresh
1 cup mayonnaise

1 cup sour cream
Salt and pepper to taste

Boil potatoes until tender. Blend lemon juice, dill, mayonnaise, sour cream, salt and pepper. Drain potatoes and cool slightly. Add to dressing. Mix gently. May leave potatoes whole if 1½ inches in diameter or cut in half.

SERVES 10-12

May add more lemon juice or dill to taste and leave skin on potatoes.

RASPBERRY-GREEN SALAD

DRESSING
½ cup raspberry vinegar
½ cup sugar

1 tablespoon seedless raspberry
   preserves
Dash of salt

½ teaspoon dry mustard
¼ cup chopped onions
½ cup vegetable oil

SALAD
2 bunches Bibb lettuce
1 bunch red leaf lettuce

1 package (8 ounce) shredded
   Monterey Jack cheese

1 cup chopped pecans
1 large bunch seedless grapes

DRESSING
Combine vinegar, sugar, preserves, salt, mustard and onions in a blender. Process and slowly add oil.

SALAD
Combine Bibb lettuce, leaf lettuce, Jack cheese, pecans and grapes. Pour on dressing and toss to coat.

SERVES 4-6

SALAD WITH BLUE CHEESE, ROASTED PEARS, BEETS AND ENDIVE

2 heads endive, split and cut into
  1 inch slices
3 pears, cut into ½ inch dice
4 medium beets, cut into ½ inch dice
2 tablespoons vegetable oil

½ teaspoon kosher salt
1 small garlic clove, minced
2 tablespoons olive oil
2 tablespoons walnut oil
1 tablespoon cider vinegar

Pepper to taste
1 teaspoon kosher salt
10 cups baby spinach leaves
6 ounces blue goat cheese or
  mild blue cheese

Toss together endive, pears, beets, vegetable oil and salt. Transfer to a roasting pan. Roast at 375 degrees, shaking pan frequently, about 20-35 minutes. Remove from oven.

Combine garlic, olive oil, walnut oil, vinegar, pepper and salt in a blender. Process until smooth. Place spinach in a large bowl. Pour on dressing and toss to coat. Divide spinach among 4 plates. Top each plate with roasted pears and vegetables. Divide blue cheese among plates.

SERVES 4

SPINACH SALAD

DRESSING

1 cup vegetable oil	¼ cup white vinegar	¾ cup sugar
⅓ cup ketchup	1 teaspoon salt	1 medium onion, chopped
2 teaspoons Worcestershire sauce		

SALAD

1 package spinach	Bacon, cooked and crumbled	3 hard-cooked eggs, chopped
1 red onion, chopped		

DRESSING

Combine oil, ketchup, Worcestershire sauce, vinegar, salt, sugar and onions in a blender. Process until smooth.

SALAD

Combine spinach, onions, bacon and eggs in a serving bowl. Pour on dressing and toss to coat.

SERVES 4

SPRING PEA/BEAN SALAD

1 cup fresh or frozen edamame, shelled
1 cup fresh or frozen green peas
1 cup fresh or frozen lima beans
1 lemon, zested

1 lemon, juiced
3 tablespoons white wine vinegar
2 green onions, minced
2 tablespoons chopped mint
1 tablespoon chopped chives

¼ cup extra virgin olive oil
Sea salt and pepper to taste
1 ounce shaved pecorino cheese
Mint for garnish

Cook edamame in boiling salted water for 2 minutes or until crisp-tender. Remove with a wire mesh strainer and plunge in ice water. Save cooking water. Drain edamame and set aside. Return water to boiling. Cook peas 4 minutes and repeat draining process. Repeat with lima beans, cooking about 5 minutes. Combine lemon zest, lemon juice, vinegar, green onions, mint and chives. Whisk in oil. Sprinkle with salt and pepper. Place edamame, peas and beans in a bowl. Pour on vinaigrette. Top with pecorino cheese and garnish with mint.

SERVES 4

STACY SCOTT'S ALMOST FAMOUS WILD RICE AND CHICKEN SALAD

1 package (6 ounce) long-grain and wild rice mix
¾-1 pound boneless skinless chicken breast halves, cooked and cubed

¾ cup red seedless grapes, halved
¾ cup sliced celery
¾ cup cashews
½ teaspoon salt

¾ cup mayonnaise
1 tablespoon milk
3 tablespoons lemon juice

Prepare rice according to package directions. Cool. Combine rice, chicken, grapes, celery and cashews. Blend salt, mayonnaise, milk and lemon juice. Pour on dressing and toss to coat. Refrigerate.

SERVES 4-6

Cashews become soft if refrigerated a long time. If preparing the day in advance. Add cashews before serving.

❤ TOMATO, AVOCADO SALAD WITH LIME, TOASTED CUMIN AND CILANTRO VINAIGRETTE

VINAIGRETTE

¼ cup lime juice

2 tablespoons rice wine vinegar

1 tablespoon honey

1 tablespoon cumin seeds, lightly toasted

¼ cup chopped cilantro

¼ cup olive oil

¼ cup canola oil

Salt and pepper to taste

SALAD

4 large tomatoes, cut into 1 inch chunks or 20 cherry tomatoes, halved

2 ripe large Hass avocados, halved, pitted, peeled and cut into 1 inch chunks

1 large red onion, thinly sliced

2 cups arugula leaves

1 teaspoon ground cumin

¼ cup chopped cilantro

VINAIGRETTE

Whisk together lime juice, vinegar, honey, cumin seeds and cilantro. Gradually whisk in olive oil and canola oil until emulsified. Add salt and pepper. Do not use blender.

SALAD

Gently combine tomatoes, avocados, red onions, arugula and half the vinaigrette. Check seasoning and add more vinaigrette as needed. Toss to coat. Sprinkle with cumin and cilantro. Serve immediately.

SERVES 4-6

❤ TABBOULEH SALAD

1 cup bulghur wheat
1 cup boiling water
2 medium tomatoes, chopped
4 green onions, thinly sliced

¼ cup minced parsley
¼-½ cup chopped mint
½ teaspoon lemon zest
⅓ cup lemon juice

3 tablespoons olive oil
½ teaspoon salt
½ teaspoon pepper
Lettuce leaves

Place bulghur in a large bowl. Pour on hot water. Cover and let stand 30 minutes. Stir in tomatoes, green onions, parsley, mint, lemon zest, lemon juice, oil, salt and pepper. Refrigerate 1 hour. Spoon mixture over lettuce leaves.

SERVES 4-6

AMERICAN BLUE CHEESE DRESSING

1 large garlic clove
1 teaspoon kosher salt
1 teaspoon dry mustard
1 teaspoon lemon juice

1 tablespoon balsamic vinegar
2 tablespoons light olive oil
⅔ cup sour cream
2 tablespoons homemade
   mayonnaise

2 green onions, finely chopped
3 ounces blue cheese
Pepper to taste

Mash together garlic and salt until a paste forms. Transfer to a bowl. Stir in dry mustard. Whisk in lemon juice and vinegar. Slowly whisk in oil. In a separate bowl, blend sour cream and mayonnaise. Whisk into oil mixture. Add green onions, blue cheese and pepper.

SERVES 1 CUP

 # BASIL PURÉE

2 ounces basil leaves
3 garlic cloves

½ teaspoon salt

1 cup olive oil

Rinse basil and remove stems. Purée garlic in food processor. Add basil, salt and oil. Purée mixture until smooth. Refrigerate.

SERVES 2 CUPS

BROWN SUGAR VINAIGRETTE

6 garlic cloves
1 cup white vinegar
1½ teaspoons Dijon mustard

1 tablespoon salt
½ cup mayonnaise
1 cup brown sugar

1½ teaspoons pepper
2¼ cups canola oil

Chop garlic in a food processor. Add vinegar, mustard, salt, mayonnaise, brown sugar and pepper. Process until smooth. Slowly add oil in a steady stream until emulsified. Refrigerate.

SERVES 5 CUPS

DIJON BLUE CHEESE DRESSING

2¼ cups mayonnaise

1 cup milk

¼ cup Dijon mustard

1 teaspoon lemon juice

¼ teaspoon paprika

1 teaspoon garlic salt

7 ounces blue cheese

Whisk together mayonnaise, milk, mustard, lemon juice, paprika and garlic salt. Add blue cheese. Refrigerate.

SERVES ABOUT 2 CUPS

DIJON-DILL MUSTARD DRESSING

¾ cup cider vinegar

1 teaspoon salt

2 heaping tablespoons Dijon mustard

1 tablespoon dried minced onions

1 teaspoon dried dill

¼ teaspoon garlic powder

1 tablespoon dried parsley

¼ teaspoon pepper

1½ cups vegetable oil

Combine vinegar, salt, mustard, onions, dill, garlic powder, parsley and pepper in a blender. Blend until smooth. Slowly add oil until emulsified.

SERVES 2 CUPS

DRESSING FOR AVOCADO-GRAPEFRUIT SALAD

1½ tablespoons grapefruit juice   ⅓ cup vegetable oil   Salt and pepper to taste
1½ tablespoons lemon juice

Blend grapefruit juice, lemon juice, oil, salt and pepper until smooth.

SERVES ½ CUP

GREEK SALAD DRESSING

1 tablespoon herbs de provence   1⅓ cups olive oil   1⅓ cups canola oil
1⅓ cups balsamic vinegar

Blend herbs, vinegar, olive oil and canola oil. Store at room temperature. Dressing will separate. Shake before using.

SERVES ABOUT 4 CUPS

SOUPS AND SANDWICHES

A BRUNSWICK STEW

3 boneless skinless chicken breast halves, cut into 2 inch pieces

3 boneless skinless thighs, cut into 2 inch pieces

1 small pork tenderloin, sliced into 2 inch pieces

1 onion, chopped

1 package (10 ounce) frozen lima beans

1 package (10 ounce) frozen whole kernel corn

1 can (16 ounce) diced tomatoes

½ cup packed brown sugar

½ cup ketchup

1 teaspoon Tabasco sauce

½ cup vinegar

½ cup Worcestershire sauce

Combine chicken, pork, onions, lima beans, corn and tomatoes in a crock pot or large stockpot. Stir in brown sugar, ketchup, Tabasco, vinegar and Worcestershire sauce. Cook several hours on low heat. Serve with bread and applesauce.

SERVES 10-12

H DOROTHY SULLIVAN
FORMER ASSOCIATE HEAD OF SCHOOL

CHEESY CHICKEN CORN CHOWDER

3 cans (10 ounces each) cream of chicken soup, undiluted

1 can (14 ounce) chicken broth

1 package (16 ounce) frozen whole kernel corn

2 cups cooked and chopped chicken breast

½ can (10 ounce) diced tomatoes with green chilies

1 can (8 ounce) cream-style corn

1 package (8 ounce) processed cheese loaf

1 garlic clove, minced

¼ teaspoon pepper

Blend soup and broth. Add kernel corn, chicken, tomatoes, creamed corn, cheese, garlic and pepper. Bring to boil. Reduce heat and simmer, uncovered, 30 minutes, stirring often. May be frozen for up to 1 month.

SERVES 6

♥ AUTHENTIC SKYLINE CHILI

1 pound ground sirloin
1 large onion, finely chopped
1 tablespoon olive oil
1 teaspoon garlic powder
½ teaspoon cinnamon
½ teaspoon ground allspice
    (may omit allspice and double
    cinnamon)

½ teaspoon crushed red pepper
1 teaspoon steak sauce
3 tablespoons chili powder
1 tablespoon white vinegar
½ ounce semi-sweet chocolate
    baking square (optional)
1 can (15 ounce) tomato sauce
3 bay leaves

3 cups water
Salt to taste
Vermicelli, cooked al dente
Shredded Cheddar cheese, finely
    chopped sweet onions, oyster
    crackers and Tabasco sauce for
    garnish

Brown meat and onions in oil. Add garlic powder, cinnamon, allspice, red pepper, steak sauce, chili powder, vinegar, chocolate, tomato sauce, bay leaves and water. Simmer, uncovered, 2 hours. May use a splatter screen. Add salt. Serve over vermicelli and top with garnish of choice. Cool completely before placing in refrigerator or freezer.

SERVES 4-6

Best prepared a day in advance. May add kidney beans during last 30 minutes of cooking.

BEEF STEW WITH DUMPLINGS

1-2 tablespoons canola oil
1 pound cubed stew beef
1 medium yellow onions, sliced
4-5 cups water
1 bay leaf

1 teaspoon sugar
1 teaspoon lemon juice
1 teaspoon Worcestershire sauce
Salt and pepper to taste

3-4 carrots, peeled and sliced into
  rounds and sticks
3-4 medium red potatoes, peeled
  and cubed
Biscuit baking mix

Heat oil in a large stockpot. Brown beef cubes. Add onions. Cook and stir until slightly browned. Add water, bay leaf, sugar, lemon juice, Worcestershire sauce, salt and pepper. Reduce heat, cover and simmer 1 hour, 30 minutes-2 hours. Remove cover. Add carrots and potatoes. Increase heat to boiling. Add salt. Cook about 20 minutes. Prepare dumplings according to baking mix directions. Add dumplings to stew and cook as directed. Add more water if needed. Remove bay leaf before serving.

SERVES 4-6

Stew is great to keep warm and serve as people are ready to eat. This recipe has been handed down for four generations so far. It is even better the second day and is easy to prepare. Store in refrigerator.

CARROT SOUP

1 stick butter
10 large organic carrots, coarsely
  chopped
1 medium onion, coarsely chopped

1 teaspoon salt
3 tablespoons chopped dill or to
  taste

10 cups chicken broth
⅓ cup rice
Dill sprigs for garnish

Melt butter in stockpot. Add carrots and onions. Cover and sauté 5 minutes. Stir in salt, dill, broth and rice. Cook until rice is tender. Purée in batches in a blender. Top with dill sprig. Serve warm or cold.

SERVES 6-8

BOB'S CHILI

2½-3 pounds ground beef
3 teaspoons canola oil
1-2 bell peppers, chopped
2 cans (7 ounces each) mushrooms
2 large onions
2 cans (6 ounces each) tomato paste
1 cup red wine
1 can (12 ounce) beer

2 cans (15 ounces each) red kidney
  beans
1 teaspoon dried thyme
1 teaspoon dried oregano
1 teaspoon ground cumin
2 cans (16 ounces each) diced
  tomatoes
1 tablespoon brown sugar
3 tablespoons chili mix

1 tablespoon salsa with jalapeños
2 tablespoons Worcestershire sauce
1 tablespoon steak sauce
1 tablespoon salt
1 teaspoon pepper
3 garlic cloves, chopped
½ square semi-sweet baking
  chocolate

Brown beef in a large stockpot. Drain beef and remove from pot. Heat oil in pot. Sauté peppers, mushrooms and onions until tender. Return beef. Add tomato paste, wine, beer, kidney beans, thyme, oregano, cumin, tomatoes, brown sugar, chili mix, salsa, Worcestershire sauce, steak sauce, salt, pepper, garlic and chocolate. Cook 1-2 hours.

SERVES 12

Chili is better made a day in advance.

CHICKEN AND COCONUT MILK SOUP

2 cups coconut cream

1 cup coconut milk

2 stalks lemongrass, white part only, cut into 1 inch pieces

1 x ½ inch piece galangal, thinly sliced

2 tablespoons coarsely chopped shallots

10-15 small chili peppers, halved lengthwise

¼-½ pound straw mushrooms, rinsed, drained and halved

12 ounces boneless skinless chicken breasts, thinly sliced

2-3 tablespoons fish sauce or to taste

3 kaffir lime leaves, stemmed

½ cup coarsely chopped cilantro

2 tablespoons lime juice

2 green onions, chopped for garnish

Combine coconut cream, coconut milk, lemongrass, galangal, shallots, chilies and mushrooms in a wok or saucepan over high heat. Bring to boil. Reduce heat and simmer 3 to 5 minutes. Stir in chicken. Add fish sauce and lime leaves. Return to boil. Add half cilantro and turn off heat. Stir in lime juice. Ladle into serving bowls. Garnish with green onions and remaining cilantro.

SERVES 4-6

For a less rich soup, replace coconut cream with an equal quantity of coconut milk. For a less spicy broth, keep chili peppers whole.

CHILI BLANCO

1 pound Northern white beans
10 cups chicken broth
2 garlic cloves, minced
2 medium onions, chopped
1 tablespoon vegetable oil

2 cans (4 ounces each) sliced green chilies
3 cups canned tomatoes and juice
2 teaspoons ground cumin
1½ teaspoons dried oregano
¼ teaspoon ground cloves

¼ teaspoon cayenne pepper
4 cups cooked and diced chicken
Grated Monterey Jack cheese for garnish
Salt and pepper to taste

Soak beans overnight in water. Drain. Combine beans, broth, garlic and half onions. Bring to boil. Reduce heat and simmer about 2 hours until beans are tender.

Sauté remaining onions in oil until tender. Add green chilies, tomatoes and juice, cumin, oregano, cloves and cayenne. Mix well. Add to bean mixture. Add chicken and simmer 1 hour. Top with Jack cheese. Sprinkle with salt and pepper.

SERVES 14-16

Delicious cold weather soup. Great for large group of people. Serve with warm cornbread.

Coach and Six Black Bean Soup

4 cups dried black beans
3 quarts cold water
3 quarts chicken broth
1 stick butter
3 onions, minced

4 stalks celery, minced
2 medium carrots, diced
2 bell peppers, diced
3 tablespoons all-purpose flour
Salt and pepper to taste

1 cup Madeira
5 cups cooked yellow rice
Chopped onions, thinly sliced lemon
    and sour cream for garnish

Soak beans in cold water overnight. Drain beans. Cook beans in broth about 2 hours. Melt butter in skillet. Sauté onions, celery, carrots and peppers until lightly browned and tender. Sprinkle flour over vegetable mixture. Toss to coat and cook 2 minutes. Sprinkle with salt and pepper.

Drain cooked beans, reserving liquid. Combine beans and vegetable mixture. Purée in batches in blender or food processor. Transfer to stockpot. Add reserved cooking liquid. Mix well. Simmer until thoroughly heated. Stir in Madeira. Garnish each serving with ½ cup rice, onions, lemon slices and dollop sour cream.

Serves 10

 Instant Black Bean Soup

2 cans (15 ounce) no salt black
    beans, undrained
½ cup bottled salsa
1 tablespoon chili powder

1 can (16 ounce) fat free reduced
    salt chicken broth
½ cup shredded reduced fat sharp
    Cheddar cheese

5 tablespoons low fat sour cream
5 tablespoons minced green onions
2½ tablespoons chopped cilantro

Place black beans in a medium saucepan. Partially mash beans with a potato masher. Place over high heat. Stir in salsa, chili powder and chicken broth. Bring to boil. Ladle soup into five bowls. Top each bowl with 1½ tablespoons Cheddar cheese, 1 tablespoon sour cream, 1 tablespoon onions and 1½ teaspoons cilantro.

Serves 5

Serve with toasted tortilla wedges.

COOL N' SPICY GREEN TOMATO SOUP
WITH CRAB AND COUNTRY HAM

½ cup vegetable oil

5 ounces country ham, julienned

2 medium onions, thinly sliced

Salt and pepper to taste

6 whole garlic cloves

2 bay leaves

2 jalapeños, stemmed and sliced

4 green anaheim peppers

2 green pasilla chilies

3½ pounds firm green tomatoes, cored and cut into eighths

1½ quarts chicken broth

3 tablespoons lemon juice

1½ tablespoons Tabasco sauce

Salt to taste

1 pound lump crabmeat, picked over for cartilage

1½ cups sour cream

1 cup tomatoes, peeled, seeded and chopped

6 tablespoons capers

½ cup chopped green onions

Heat oil in a large stockpot. Cook ham about 2 minutes until golden browned. Remove from heat. Remove ham with a slotted spoon. Heat reserved oil. Sauté onions about 3-4 minutes until tender. Add salt and pepper. Add garlic, bay leaves, jalapeños, anaheims and pasilla chilies. Cook 5 minutes. Add tomatoes and broth. Add salt and pepper. Bring to boil. Reduce heat and simmer 15 minutes until tomatoes are tender. Remove bay laves. Purée mixture with a hand held blender until smooth. Refrigerate soup.

Stir in lemon juice, Tabasco and salt. Combine crabmeat, sour cream, tomatoes, capers and green onions in a bowl. Sprinkle salad with salt and pepper. Ladle soup into individual soup bowls. Serve with crabmeat salad and crisp ham. May serve soup warm or cold.

SERVES 12

Creamy Tortilla Soup

3 tablespoons butter
1 onion, chopped
1 can (4 ounce) chopped green
  chilies
2 cans (16 ounces each) diced
  tomatoes

½ jar (14 ounce) artichoke hearts,
  chopped
6 ounces cream cheese, softened
1 can (14 ounce) chicken broth
1½ cups half-and-half
¼ cup lemon juice
1 cup grilled chopped chicken

1 avocado, chopped
Garlic powder, cayenne pepper,
  ground cumin, salt and pepper
  to taste
Shredded Monterey Jack cheese
  for garnish
Tortilla chips

Melt butter in a large stockpot. Sauté onions until tender. Add green chilies, tomatoes and artichokes. Cook until most liquid evaporates. Stir in cream cheese until cheese melts. Add broth, half-and-half, lemon juice and chicken. Stir in garlic powder, cayenne, cumin, salt and pepper. Heat thoroughly. Do not boil. Add avocado. Top each serving with Jack cheese. Serve with chips.

SERVES 4

Curried Avocado Soup

2 tablespoons diced onions
1 tablespoon butter
1 tablespoon curry powder
3 cups chicken broth

3 avocados, peeled and pitted
1 teaspoon salt
3-4 drops Tabasco sauce

2 cups sour cream
6-8 lime or lemon slices
2 tablespoons chopped parsley

Sauté onions in butter until tender. Stir in curry. Cook about 3 minutes. Add broth. Bring to boil. Remove from heat. Purée avocados in blender. Slowly add broth, salt and Tabasco. Blend until smooth. Refrigerate. Just before serving, fold in sour cream. Ladle soup into serving bowls. Top with lime or lemon slices and parsley.

SERVES 6

HEARTY CORN CHOWDER

3 tablespoons butter
1 cup chopped carrots
1 cup chopped celery
⅓ cup finely chopped onions
3 tablespoons all-purpose flour
2 cups water
½ teaspoon salt

½ teaspoon celery salt
¼ teaspoon paprika
⅛ teaspoon pepper
1 can (12 ounce) whole kernel corn
    with sweet red bell peppers
2½ cups shredded sharp Cheddar
    cheese

½ pound smoked sausage, cut into
    ¼ inch slices
1 can (14½ ounce) evaporated skim
    milk
Snipped parsley for garnish

Cook butter, carrots, celery and onions in a large stockpot until bubbly. Cover and reduce heat. Simmer, stirring occasionally, 20 minutes. Stir in flour. Cook over low heat, stirring constantly, until bubbly. Add water, salt, celery salt, paprika, pepper and corn. Heat to boiling. Gradually stir in Cheddar cheese until cheese melts. Add sausage and milk. Heat until hot. Top with parsley.

SERVES 6-8

ONION SOUP WITH WHITE WINE

6 tablespoons butter
4 large onions, finely chopped
3 cups chicken broth
1 cup dry white wine

Salt and pepper to taste
Large croutons, toasted in butter
    or oil

Mixture of grated Gruyère and
    Parmesan cheese
Chopped onions and chopped
    parsley for garnish

Melt butter in a stockpot. Add onions. Cover tightly and steam over low heat until tender. Add broth and wine. Simmer 15-20 minutes. Add salt and pepper.

Sprinkle croutons with cheese mixture. Broil croutons to melt cheese. To serve, place croutons in bottom of individual bowls. Ladle soup on top. Top with onions and parsley.

SERVES 6

♡ QUICK VEGETABLE SOUP

1 pound ground beef
1 garlic clove, minced
1 cup chopped onions
2 cups coarsely chopped cabbage

1 can (16 ounce) mixed vegetables, drained
1 can (28 ounce) tomatoes, chopped, undrained
1 can (8 ounce) tomato sauce

2½ teaspoons salt
¼ teaspoon pepper
2 cups water
1 cup shell macaroni
½ cup grated Parmesan cheese

Brown ground beef. Add garlic, onions, cabbage, vegetables, tomatoes with juice, tomato sauce, salt, pepper and water. Bring to boil. Add macaroni. Reduce heat and simmer 15 minutes. Remove from heat. Top each serving with Parmesan cheese.

SERVES 6-8

May prepare this soup early in the day and add macaroni before serving. May also reheat before serving. Freezes well.

VICHYSSOISE

2 cups finely diced potatoes
4 tablespoons butter
6 leeks, cleaned and cut into
    1 inch pieces

3 cups chicken broth
1 teaspoon salt
½ teaspoon pepper
Dash of ground nutmeg

1½-2 cups sour cream or heavy cream
Chopped chives for garnish

Cover potatoes with salted water. Cook until tender. Drain and cool. Melt butter in skillet. Cook leeks, tossing gently, for 5 minutes. Add broth and bring to boil. Reduce heat and simmer leeks until tender. Add potatoes, salt, pepper and nutmeg. Purée in blender in batches, blending 1 minute until smooth. Refrigerate. When ready to serve, stir in sour cream. Top with chives.

SERVES 6

SMOKED SALMON BISQUE

4 tablespoons butter
⅓ cup all-purpose flour
1 quart vegetable broth
1 quart half-and-half

½ cup sherry
1 tablespoon Worcestershire sauce
2 teaspoons lemon juice
1 teaspoon Tabasco sauce

½ teaspoon garlic salt
¼ teaspoon white pepper
8 ounces smoked salmon, finely chopped

Melt butter in Dutch oven. Whisk in flour and cook, stirring continuously, for 5 minutes until smooth. Gradually whisk in broth. Bring to boil. Reduce heat and simmer 10 minutes. Add half-and-half, sherry, Worcestershire sauce, lemon juice, Tabasco, garlic salt and pepper. Cook until warm. Add salmon.

SERVES 3 QUARTS

May top bisque with rosemary sprigs.

SPINACH AND LENTIL SOUP

1½ cups dry brown lentils
6 cups cold water
1 bunch English spinach, well rinsed
¼ cup olive oil

1 large yellow onion, finely chopped
3 garlic cloves, finely chopped
3 tablespoons chopped cilantro
Salt and pepper to taste

¼ cup lemon juice
Extra-virgin olive oil and lemon wedges for garnish
Pita or bread of choice

Rinse lentils in a sieve under cold running water. Place in a heavy saucepan with cold water. Bring to boil. Reduce heat, cover and simmer 25-30 minutes until lentils are tender. Skim surface if necessary. Slice spinach down the middle and coarsely shred. In a separate heavy saucepan, heat olive oil over medium-low heat. Sauté onions until tender. Add garlic and sauté a few seconds. Add spinach and cook until wilted. Add spinach mixture to lentils. Add cilantro, salt, pepper and lemon juice. Cover and simmer 10 minutes more. Ladle soup into deep bowls and drizzle with oil. Serve with lemon wedges and bread.

SERVES 5-6

SPAGHETTI SOUP

½ pound bulk sausage
½ pound ground beef
1 cup chopped onions
2 garlic cloves, minced

1 can (28 ounce) Italian style tomatoes with basil, coarsely chopped with juice
2 cups beef broth
1 cup tomato juice
1 teaspoon salt

¼ teaspoon dried basil
¼ teaspoon dried oregano
1 bay leaf
¼ cup chopped parsley
1 cup broken spaghetti noodles
Grated Parmesan cheese

Cook sausage, beef, onions and garlic about 10 minutes in a large stockpot, stirring to break up meat. Drain drippings from pot. Add tomatoes with juice, broth, tomato juice, salt, basil, oregano, bay leaf, parsley and spaghetti. Cover and simmer about 30 minutes until flavors blend. Remove bay leaf. Ladle into soup bowls and top with Parmesan cheese.

SERVES 4

Quick and easy for a great weeknight meal. Serve with green salad and garlic bread. May double recipe.

TOMATO SOUP

2 pounds tomatoes, peeled
2 teaspoons extra-virgin olive oil
2 garlic cloves, finely chopped
1 yellow onion, finely chopped
1 stalk celery, finely chopped

4 cups vegetable broth
1 tablespoon tomato paste
½ teaspoon sugar
Salt and pepper to taste

1 bay leaf
1 tablespoon chopped basil
1 tablespoon chopped oregano
1 tablespoon chopped parsley

Purée tomatoes in a food processor. Pour into a bowl through a sieve to remove seeds. Heat olive oil and garlic in a saucepan about 1 minute until fragrant. Add onions and celery. Cook until tender. Add tomato purée, broth, tomato paste, sugar, salt, pepper and bay leaf. Simmer about 20 minutes. Remove bay leaf. Add basil, oregano and parsley. Cook 5-10 minutes more until slightly thickened. Serve immediately.

SERVES 4

SPLIT PEA AND HAM SOUP

2½ cups dry green or yellow
    split peas
8 cups cold water
1 meaty ham bone

2 whole cloves
1 large yellow onion, finely
    chopped

2 carrots, peeled and finely
    chopped
Ground pepper to taste

Sort peas and discard any discolored peas. Rinse peas in a colander under cold running water. Place peas in a large heavy saucepan. Add water, ham bone, cloves, onions and carrots. Slowly bring to boil. Reduce heat, cover and simmer gently for 1 hour until meat begins to fall from bone. Remove bone with tongs and cool. Remove meat from bone and chop. Discard bone. Blend soup in a food processor, working in batches. Return mixture to saucepan. Add meat. Cover and simmer about 1 hour, stirring occasionally or until peas are tender and soup is desired consistency. Sprinkle with pepper. May top with croutons.

SERVES 6-8

VINALHAVEN CORN CHOWDER

½ cup diced bacon
2 cups diced Vidalia onions
2 large carrots, diced to ¼ inch
1 stalk celery, diced to ¼ inch
1 sweet red pepper, finely diced
2 small Yukon Gold potatoes,
    peeled and diced to ¼ inch

1 medium sweet potato, diced to
    ¼ inch
5 cups reduced sodium chicken
    broth
6 ears sweet corn, cut from cob
2 sprigs thyme

1½ cups heavy cream
1 teaspoon fine sea salt
1 teaspoon pepper
2 plum tomatoes, seeded and diced
    for garnish

Cook bacon in stockpot until crisp. Transfer to paper towel. Sauté onions, carrots, celery and pepper in drippings. Add Gold potatoes, sweet potatoes and broth. Simmer until vegetables are tender. Add corn, thyme and cream. Simmer an additional 10 minutes. Stir in salt, pepper and bacon. Top each serving with tomatoes.

SERVES 6

May use food processor to chop all vegetables. May substitute half-and-half for heavy cream.

TEXAS CHILI

6 tablespoons vegetable oil

3 pounds round steak, cut into
 ½ inch cubes

6 tablespoons chili powder

6 tablespoons all-purpose flour

1 teaspoon cumin seeds

1 teaspoon dried oregano

1 teaspoon salt

3 garlic cloves, minced

2 cans (14 ounces each) beef broth

Heat oil in a skillet until smoking hot. Brown meat, stirring constantly. Stir in chili powder and flour. Add cumin seeds, oregano, salt, garlic and broth. Mix well. Bring to simmer. Cover and cook 4-6 hours or more. Do not boil. May cook up to 24 hours.

SERVES 6

May serve over rice or with shredded lettuce, chopped onions and shredded Cheddar cheese. Other toppings are sliced black olives, guacamole, sliced jalapeños, chopped tomatoes, tortilla chips.

To prepare in crock pot, trim meat well and do not add oil. Combine meat, all dry ingredients and garlic. Mix well. Add enough broth just to cover meat. Place on high until hot. Reduce heat to low. Cover and cook overnight. Place cover partially off to allow liquid to evaporate and sauce will thicken. Skim off fat accumulated on top.

WEEK NIGHT QUICK CHICKEN CHILI

1 small onion, diced
2 garlic cloves, minced
1 can (14½ ounce) chicken broth
2 cans (14-16 ounces each) diced tomatoes
1 can (10 ounce) diced tomatoes with green chilies

1 can (4 ounce) diced green chilies (optional)
½ teaspoon dried oregano
½ teaspoon dried coriander
¼ teaspoon ground cumin
2 cans (10 ounces each) chicken breast

1 can (15 ounce) white navy beans
1 cup frozen corn
Lime wedges, shredded Cheddar cheese, avocado slices, sour cream and tortilla strips for garnish

Sauté onions and garlic in a Dutch oven or stockpot. Stir in broth, tomatoes, tomatoes with green chilies, green chilies, oregano, coriander and cumin. Bring to boil. Reduce heat and simmer 10 minutes. Add chicken, beans and corn. Return to boil. Reduce heat and simmer an additional 5 minutes.

SERVES 4-6

I have never added the optional green chilies and the soup is mildly spicy. I love this soup served cold the next day! This dish goes well with cornbread. It is relatively low calorie and low fat. Freezes well.

BARBECUE SANDWICHES

1 (3 pound) boneless pork loin roast, trimmed
1 cup water
1 bottle (18 ounce) barbecue sauce

¼ cup firmly packed brown sugar
2 tablespoons Worcestershire sauce
1-2 tablespoons Tabasco sauce
1 teaspoon salt

½ teaspoon pepper
Hamburger buns
Coleslaw

Place roast in a 4 quart slow cooker. Add water. Cover and cook on high 7 hours or until meat is tender. Shred meat with a fork. Combine meat, barbecue sauce, brown sugar, Worcestershire sauce, Tabasco, salt and pepper in slow cooker. Reduce heat to low. Cover and cook 1 hour. Serve barbecue meat on buns with coleslaw.

SERVES 8

BLT BITES

16-20 large cherry tomatoes
1 pound bacon, cooked and
  crumbled

½ cup mayonnaise
⅓ cup diced onions
3 tablespoons Parmesan cheese

2 tablespoons finely chopped
  parsley

Wash tomatoes and slice a thin section off bottom. Scoop out pulp and invert onto paper towels to drain. Combine bacon, mayonnaise, onions, Parmesan cheese and parsley. Spoon mixture into tomatoes. Refrigerate at least 2 hours.

SERVES 10

CHEESE SANDWICHES

2 cups grated Cheddar cheese
½ cup finely chopped pecans
½ cup mayonnaise

1 tablespoon grated yellow onion
¼ teaspoon pepper
⅛ teaspoon cayenne pepper

1 loaf (1 pound) thinly sliced white
  bread

Combine Cheddar cheese, pecans, mayonnaise, onions, pepper and cayenne. Mix well. Spread a thin layer of mayonnaise on one side of each bread slice. Spread cheese mixture over half bread slices. Top with remaining bread slices. Trim edges. Cut into triangles or fingers if desired.

SERVES 12-15

CHICKEN APPLE PANINI

1 can (12 ounce) dark and light
  chicken meat, drained
½ cup mayonnaise
1 tablespoon lemon juice

1½ cups grated Swiss cheese
2 stalks celery, chopped
1 apple, finely chopped

½ cup grated carrot
12 slices whole wheat bread
2 tablespoons butter

Combine chicken, mayonnaise, lemon juice, Swiss cheese, celery, apples and carrots. Mix well. Divide mixture and make six sandwiches. Spread butter on outside bread slices. Grill sandwiches, covered, over medium heat, turning once until cheese melts and bread is toasted. For indoor grilling, cook on dual-contact grill 3-5 minutes until bread is golden browned.

SERVES 6

This sandwich cooks beautifully either on a nonstick skillet or in a George Foreman dual sided indoor grill.

SMOKED GOUDA AND PROSCIUTTO PANINI SANDWICHES

2 slices sourdough bread
2 tablespoons olive oil or butter,
  melted

2 ounces sliced smoked gouda
2 ounces thinly sliced prosciutto
2 tablespoons thinly sliced red
  onions

2 tomato slices
1 ounce shredded Fontina cheese

Brush both sides of bread with oil or butter. Assemble sandwich layers in order with gouda, prosciutto, onions, tomato slice and Fontina cheese. Top with bread slice. Place sandwich in a Panini press or in a heated grill pan pressed down with another heavy pan. Cook until crisp and golden browned. Serve immediately.

SERVES 1

CUCUMBER MINT TEA SANDWICHES

½ cup chopped mint

4 tablespoons butter, softened

4 tablespoons cream cheese, softened

1 English cucumber, thinly sliced

Salt to taste

12 slices thin whole wheat bread

Combine mint, butter and cream cheese until smooth. Set aside. Cut a 6 inch piece of cucumber into thin slices. Spread butter mixture on bread slices. Top six bread slices with cucumber slices. Sprinkle with salt. Top with remaining six bread slices, butter side down. Cut sandwiches diagonally into quarters.

SERVES 6

ROAST BEEF AND BLUE CHEESE TEA SANDWICHES

1 cup blue cheese, crumbled

1½ cups mayonnaise

3 tablespoons lemon juice

36 slices thin whole wheat bread

3 bunches watercress

1½ pounds thinly sliced roast beef

Blend blue cheese, mayonnaise and lemon juice. Spread blue cheese mayonnaise on each bread slice. Divide watercress and roast beef among eighteen bread slices. Top with remaining eighteen bread slices, mayonnaise side down. Cut sandwiches diagonally into quarters.

SERVES 18

SMOKED SALMON-WASABI TEA SANDWICHES

3 tablespoons wasabi powder
6 teaspoons water
3 packages (8 ounces each) cream
   cheese, softened

36 slices thin whole wheat bread
24 ounces smoked salmon, thinly
   sliced

6 teaspoons lemon zest
9 tablespoons chopped cilantro

Blend wasabi and water into a paste. Beat in cream cheese until smooth. Spread wasabi mixture over bread slices. Divide salmon among eighteen bread slices. Top with lemon zest and cilantro. Top with remaining bread slices, wasabi side down. Refrigerate for at least 2 hours. Cut diagonally into quarters.

SERVES 18

SMOKED TURKEY TEA SANDWICHES

1½ cups mayonnaise
1 cup arugula, coarsely chopped
3 tablespoons shallots, minced
3 tablespoons chopped parsley

1½ teaspoons lemon zest
Salt and pepper to taste
36 slices thin white bread

2 pounds thinly sliced smoked
   turkey
90 arugula leaves

Combine mayonnaise, chopped arugula, shallots, parsley and lemon zest. Add salt and pepper. Trim crust from bread. Spread mayonnaise mixture over bread. Divide turkey among eighteen bread slices. Place 5 arugula leaves on each sandwich. Top with remaining bread slices, mayonnaise side down, pressing to adhere. Cut diagonally into quarters.

SERVES 18

Summer Pizza

1 package (10 ounce) pizza dough
2 tomatoes, thinly sliced, and patted dry

½ cup shredded mozzarella cheese
2-3 inch balls Buffalo mozzarella, sliced
20-30 basil leaves, chopped

Olive oil
Parmesan cheese
Salt and pepper to taste

Spread pizza dough out on floured surface to desired size. Bake at 350 degrees 5 minutes. Arrange tomatoes over crust. Top with shredded mozzarella cheese and sliced mozzarella cheese. Sprinkle with basil, oil, Parmesan cheese, salt and pepper. Bake until cheese melts.

SERVES 10 APPETIZER OR 5 MAIN COURSE

Taylor's Pressed Cubano Sandwiches

2 tablespoons prepared mustard
2 teaspoons minced cilantro
8 (½ inch thick) bread slices, may use Hawaiian

8 slices Swiss cheese
6 ounces thinly sliced ham
4 ounces thinly sliced turkey
4 slices bacon, cooked and halved

16 dill pickle slices
2 teaspoons extra virgin olive oil
1 garlic clove, minced

Blend mustard and cilantro. Spread mustard over bread slices. Layer onto four bread slices in order: the Swiss cheese, ham, turkey, bacon and pickles. Top with remaining bread slices, mustard side down. Blend oil and garlic. Spread on one side of sandwich. Place oil face down on hot grill. Place a heavy flat iron over sandwich to compress while browning. Spread top side with oil mixture. Flip sandwiches and cook until browned. Serve hot.

SERVES 4

PASTA

CARRIE ELLA'S SOUR CREAM LASAGNA

1½ pounds ground chuck
¾ teaspoon salt
¼ teaspoon pepper
1½ tablespoons sugar
2 cans (8 ounces each) tomato sauce

2 cans water
1 bunch green onions, finely chopped
1 package (3 ounce) cream cheese, softened

1 container (8 ounce) sour cream
9-12 lasagna noodles, cooked al dente
½ cup grated mozzarella cheese

Brown meat. Add salt, pepper, sugar, tomato sauce and water. Simmer 15 minutes. Combine green onions, cream cheese and sour cream. Layer noodles in bottom of 13 x 9 x 2-inch baking dish. Top with sour cream mixture and then meat sauce. Repeat to make three layers, ending with meat sauce. Sprinkle with mozzarella cheese.

Bake, uncovered, at 350 degrees 20 minutes. Cool 10 minutes. Cut into squares and serve.

SERVES 8

May prepare in advance and refrigerate. Bake 45 minutes when cold. Dish also freezes well. Bake until edges are bubbly.

For low fat version, substitute ground turkey, use low fat or no fat cheese and sour cream. May also use whole wheat noodles.

This recipe is a gift from Linda de Saca and is originally from her grandmother, Carrie Ella Mountain. Please give Mrs. Mountain credit anytime this dish is praised.

CONCERT PASTA SALAD

1 teaspoon olive oil
2 boneless skinless chicken breast halves
Salt and pepper to taste

1 package (8 ounce) fusilli pasta, cooked al dente
1 small onion, chopped

1 bunch broccoli, chopped
½ cup Italian dressing
½ teaspoon Creole seasoning

Drizzle oil over chicken. Sprinkle with salt and pepper. Bake at 350 degrees 20-25 minutes. Cool and cut into bite size pieces. Combine chicken, pasta, onions and broccoli. Blend Italian dressing, seasoning, salt and pepper. Pour over salad and toss to coat.

SERVES 4-6

CROCK-POT MAC & CHEESE

1 package (8 ounce) elbow
macaroni, cooked al dente and
drained
1½ cups milk
1 can (12 ounce) evaporated milk

1 egg, slightly beaten
1 package (8 ounce) shredded
Cheddar cheese
1 cup shredded extra sharp
Cheddar cheese

4 tablespoons butter, melted
1 teaspoon salt
Dash of pepper
4-5 Cheddar cheese slices
Dash of paprika

Combine pasta, milk, evaporated milk, egg, both Cheddar cheeses, butter, salt and pepper. Mix well. Pour mixture into a greased crock-pot. Top with cheese slices. Sprinkle with paprika. Cover and cook on low heat 4 hours.

SERVES 6-8

FETTUCCINE WITH SHRIMP AND TOMATOES

1 package (8 ounce) fettuccine
1 can (14 ounce) diced tomatoes,
reserving juice
1½ pounds medium shrimp, peeled
and deveined

1 teaspoon dried basil
3 garlic cloves, minced
2 tablespoons minced shallots
½ teaspoon pepper

¼ teaspoon salt
¼ cup olive oil
Grated Parmesan cheese

Cook pasta until al dente. Drain and keep warm. Drain tomatoes reserving ¼ cup juice. Sauté shrimp, tomatoes, reserved juice, basil, garlic, shallots, pepper and salt in oil 5-7 minutes or until shrimp turn pink. Spoon mixture over pasta. Sprinkle with Parmesan cheese. Serve immediately.

SERVES 4

Fettuccine with Smoked Salmon

Sea salt to taste
1 package (8 ounce) fettuccine
2 tablespoons butter
1 shallot, minced

¼ cup plus 2 tablespoons sour cream
2 tablespoons chopped flat leaf parsley

Pepper to taste
4 ounces thinly sliced smoked salmon, cut into ½ inch ribbons

Bring water and sea salt to boil in a large stockpot. Add fettuccine and cook until al dente. Drain and reserve ½ cup cooking liquid. Melt butter in a large skillet. Sauté shallots 2 minutes, stirring constantly. Add sour cream, parsley and ¼ cup cooking liquid. Add salt and pepper. Add pasta and salmon and toss well. Add up to 2 tablespoons cooking liquid if pasta is dry. Remove from heat and serve immediately.

SERVES 4

Look for wild Alaska smoked salmon for deeper color and flavor.

Linguine Carbonara

½ pound bacon, cut into 1 inch pieces
¼ cup olive oil
1 medium onion, chopped
1 cup chopped parsley

4 ounces fontina cheese, cubed
3 ounces prosciutto, cut into strips
1 pound linguine or spaghetti
4 egg yolks, slightly beaten
¾ cup warm half-and-half

1 teaspoon salt
Pepper to taste
1 cup grated Parmesan cheese
Parsley sprigs for garnish

Cook bacon until crisp in a large skillet. Drain on paper towels. Pour off drippings. Add oil and onions to skillet. Sauté onions until tender. Set aside.

Combine parsley, Fontina cheese and prosciutto. Cook linguine in Dutch oven until al dente. Drain and return to Dutch oven. Immediately stir in egg yolks. Add bacon, onions, cheese mixture, half-and-half, salt, pepper and ½ cup Parmesan cheese. Cook over low heat until thoroughly heated, stirring constantly. Transfer to serving dish. Sprinkle with ½ cup Parmesan cheese. Top with parsley. Serve immediately.

SERVES 8

LASAGNA WITH TURKEY SAUSAGE AND GOAT CHEESE

2 tablespoons olive oil
1 cup chopped yellow onions
2 garlic cloves, minced
1½ pounds sweet Italian sausage, casing removed
1 can (28 ounce) crushed tomatoes in purée
1 can (6 ounce) tomato paste
2 tablespoons chopped Italian parsley

½ cup chopped basil
1½ teaspoons salt
½ teaspoon pepper
1 package (8 ounce) lasagna noodles
1 container (15 ounce) ricotta cheese
4 ounces creamy goat cheese, crumbled

1 cup grated Parmesan cheese
1 egg, slightly beaten
2 tablespoons chopped Italian parsley
½ teaspoon salt
¼ teaspoon pepper
1 pound mozzarella, thinly sliced
¼ cup grated Parmesan cheese

Heat oil a skillet. Sauté onions until tender. Add garlic and cook 1 minute. Stir in sausage, breaking up with a fork. Cook until no longer pink. Add tomatoes, tomato paste, parsley, basil, salt and pepper. Simmer, uncovered, over medium-high heat 15-20 minutes.

Fill a large bowl with very hot tap water. Add noodles and soak 20 minutes. Drain. Combine ricotta cheese, goat cheese, Parmesan cheese, egg, parsley, salt and pepper.

Ladle one-third meat sauce into 13 x 9 x 2-inch baking dish. Add layers in order, half pasta, half mozzarella cheese, half ricotta cheese mixture and one-third meat sauce. Repeat all layers. Top with Parmesan cheese. Bake at 400 degrees 30 minutes until bubbly.

SERVES 8

This is the only lasagna I make. Kids gobble it up, but it is elegant enough for company. To make ahead, assemble lasagna and refrigerate, unbaked. Bake 30-40 minutes.

NOODLE KUGEL

1 package (1½ pounds) medium flat
   egg noodles
6 tablespoons butter
1 package (8 ounce) cream cheese,
   softened
⅓ cup sugar

¼ cup packed brown sugar
1 teaspoon cinnamon
3 eggs
1 cup whole milk
1 cup heavy apricot nectar

2 cups crushed cornflakes
6 tablespoons butter, softened
1 teaspoon cinnamon
¼ cup packed brown sugar

Boil noodles in salted water until very al dente. Drain and place in large bowl. Add butter and toss to coat. Transfer noodles
to a greased 13 x 9 x 2-inch baking dish. Combine cream cheese, sugar, brown sugar, cinnamon, eggs, milk and nectar in
a food processor. Blend until smooth. Pour mixture over noodles and mix well.

Combine cornflake crumbs, butter, cinnamon and brown sugar until crumbly. Spread topping over noodles. Bake at
350 degrees 45 minutes-1 hour. Cover with foil if top browns too quickly. Cool 15 minutes before serving.

SERVES 8

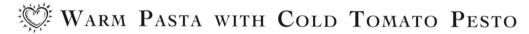

WARM PASTA WITH COLD TOMATO PESTO

3 cups chopped seeded tomatoes
½ cup chopped basil
½ cup olive oil

3 tablespoons balsamic vinegar
1 teaspoon salt
½ teaspoon pepper

2 tablespoons capers
¼ cup grated Parmesan cheese
Pasta of choice

Combine tomatoes, basil, oil, vinegar, salt, pepper, capers and Parmesan cheese. Mix well. Refrigerate several hours.
When ready to serve, cook pasta until al dente and drain. Serve cold tomato mixture over hot pasta. Top with additional
Parmesan cheese.

SERVES 4

RAY'S SHRIMP AND FETA CHEESE WITH LINGUINE

¼ cup extra virgin olive oil
2 teaspoons minced garlic
1 small onion, diced
12 jumbo shrimp, peeled and deveined

½ cup chopped tomatoes
½ cup sliced mushrooms
½ cup sliced black olives
2 tablespoons chopped basil

½ cup diced feta cheese
1 lemon wedge
Parsley for garnish
Hot cooked linguine

Heat oil in a skillet. Sauté garlic, onions and shrimp until shrimp turn pink. Add tomatoes, mushrooms, black olives and basil. Cook 2-3 minutes longer, tossing frequently. Top with feta cheese, lemon wedge and parsley. Serve with hot linguine.

SERVES 4

The perfect accompaniment is a quality French bread.

SPINACH STUFFED SHELLS

24 large pasta shells
1 jar (32 ounce) spaghetti sauce
1 package (10 ounce) frozen chopped spinach, thawed and drained

2 cups ricotta cheese
1 package (8 ounce) shredded mozzarella cheese
1 medium onion, chopped
½ cup grated Parmesan cheese

2 tablespoons chopped parsley
1 teaspoon dried oregano
3 dashes Tabasco sauce
Dash of ground nutmeg
½ cup grated Parmesan cheese

Cook shells until al dente. Spread 1 cup sauce in bottom of 13 x 9 x 2-inch baking dish. Combine spinach, ricotta cheese, mozzarella cheese, onions, Parmesan cheese, parsley, oregano, Tabasco and nutmeg. Mix well. Spoon 1½-2 tablespoons mixture into shells. Arrange shells over sauce with open side of shell facing down. Spoon remaining sauce over shells. Top with Parmesan cheese. Cover and bake at 350 degrees 30-40 minutes.

SERVES 6-8

Freezes well.

ROTINI WITH
SALMON AND ROASTED GARLIC

2 whole heads of garlic
2 tablespoons olive oil
Salt and pepper to taste
1 pound rotini or fusilli
(corkscrew shaped pasta)
½ cup Marsala or white wine

1 cup chicken broth
1 pound salmon, cut into 1 inch
cubes
1 lemon, zested
1 lemon, juiced

1 tablespoon minced rosemary
2 tablespoons extra virgin olive oil
2 tablespoons capers, drained
½ teaspoon salt
½ teaspoon pepper

Cut garlic heads in half crosswise. Place on foil. Drizzle with oil and sprinkle with salt and pepper. Fold foil up around garlic, keeping garlic flat, and seal into a tight packet. Roast at 400 degrees 1 hour until tender. Cool slightly. Squeeze cloves out of skin. Mash half garlic with a fork into a paste.

Cook pasta in salted boiling water 8-10 minutes, stirring occasionally, until al dente. Drain. Combine Marsala and broth in a heavy skillet. Bring to simmer. Add mashed garlic and stir to dissolve. Simmer, uncovered, 4 minutes. Add salmon. Cover and simmer an additional 4 minutes. Remove from heat. Add remaining roasted garlic, lemon zest, lemon juice, rosemary and cooked pasta. Mix well. Stir in oil, capers, salt and pepper. Serve immediately.

SERVES 4-6

This may seem like a lot of garlic, but because it is roasted it only contributes a mellow, nutty flavor that goes beautifully with the salmon. Capers and lemon zest add some brightness to the dish, which is a perfect light spring meal.

SPINACH LASAGNA

1 container (24 ounce) ricotta or cottage cheese

1 package (10 ounce) frozen chopped spinach, thawed and drained

1 package (8 ounce) shredded mozzarella cheese

1 egg

1 teaspoon salt

1 teaspoon dried oregano

1 jar (26 ounce) spaghetti sauce

1 package (8 ounce) lasagna noodles, uncooked

1 cup water

Combine ricotta cheese, spinach, half mozzarella cheese, egg, salt, and oregano. Mix well. Spread enough sauce to cover the bottom of greased 13 x 9 x 2-inch baking dish. Place four noodles over sauce. Spread half ricotta cheese mixture over noodles. Repeat layers of sauce, noodles and cheese mixture. Top with four more noodles, remaining sauce and mozzarella cheese.

Pour water around edges and cover tightly with foil. Bake at 350 degrees 1 hour, 15 minutes. Cool 10-15 minutes before serving.

SERVES 6-8

RIGATONI WITH VODKA SAUCE

¼ cup olive oil

1½ cups finely chopped shallots

½ teaspoon crushed red pepper

1 cup vodka

1½ cups heavy cream

1½ cups tomato sauce

1 pound penne pasta, cooked al dente and drained

8 ounces thinly sliced prosciutto, chopped

¾ cup grated Asiago cheese

¼ cup chopped Italian parsley

3 teaspoons dried basil

Salt and pepper to taste

¾ cup grated Asiago cheese

Heat oil in heavy skillet. Sauté shallots and red pepper about 5 minutes. Add vodka and ignite with a long match. Shake pan gently about 2-3 minutes until flame burns down. Increase heat to medium high. Add cream and cook 3 minutes until thickened. Stir in tomato sauce. Boil gently until thickened. Add pasta, prosciutto, Asiago cheese, parsley and basil. Sprinkle with salt and pepper. If sauce is too thick, add ¼ cup water. Top with Asiago cheese. Serve immediately.

SERVES 4

SUN-DRIED TOMATO AND BLACK OLIVE PESTO

15 sun-dried tomatoes in oil, drained

8 Kalamata olives, or other black olives, pitted

1 garlic clove

3 tablespoons whole parsley leaves

¼ cup extra virgin olive oil

½ teaspoon salt or to taste

Combine tomatoes, olives, garlic and parsley in food processor. Process, scraping down sides, until coarsely chopped. With processor running, pour in oil in a thin stream. Process to form a slightly coarse paste. Transfer pesto to a small bowl. Stir in salt. If olives are salty, may not need salt. Store in refrigerator up to 1 week.

SERVES 2-3

MUSHROOM PESTO

1 tablespoon extra virgin olive oil

1 package (10 ounce) white mushrooms, finely chopped

1 tablespoon Worcestershire sauce

1 tablespoon medium dry sherry

Salt and pepper to taste

1 garlic clove, minced

¼ teaspoon salt

¼ cup pine nuts

¼ cup grated Parmesan cheese

3 tablespoons extra virgin olive oil

½ cup packed parsley leaves, rinsed and spun dry

Heat oil in 10-12 inch nonstick skillet until hot. Sauté mushrooms with Worcestershire sauce, sherry, salt and pepper about 10 minutes until browned and liquid evaporates.

Mash garlic with salt into a paste. Purée mushroom mixture with garlic paste, pine nuts, Parmesan cheese and oil in food processor. Add parsley and blend until finely chopped. Cover surface with plastic wrap and may refrigerate up to 1 week.

SERVES 4

WEEKNIGHT SPAGHETTI PIE

6 ounces spaghetti or vermicelli
1 teaspoon dried basil
1 garlic clove, pressed
4 tablespoons butter, melted
½ cup grated Parmesan cheese
1 large egg, slightly beaten

1 cup ricotta cheese
1 pound ground beef
½ cup chopped onions
1 teaspoon dried basil
1 can (15 ounce) tomato sauce

1 can (6 ounce) tomato paste
1 teaspoon dried oregano
1 cup sliced mushrooms
¼ cup white wine (optional)
6 ounces sliced mozzarella cheese

Combine spaghetti, basil, butter, Parmesan cheese and egg. Press mixture into a lightly greased 10 inch glass pie plate. Spread ricotta cheese over top.

Cook beef and onions in a skillet, stirring to crumble meat. Drain well. Add basil, tomato sauce, tomato paste, oregano and mushrooms. Stir in wine. Cook 5 minutes or until thoroughly heated. Spoon beef mixture over ricotta cheese. Bake at 350 degrees 25 minutes. Remove from oven and top with mozzarella cheese slices. Bake an additional 5 minutes until cheese melts.

SERVES 6

GREEN OLIVE AND WALNUT PESTO

½ cup walnuts pieces or pecans

1 cup pitted green olives, if stuffed, remove pimentos

½ cup chopped parsley, stemmed

6 green onions, cut into 2 inch pieces

3 tablespoons lemon juice or to taste

¼ teaspoon crushed red pepper

¼ cup olive oil

½ cup grated Parmesan cheese

Spread walnuts in a shallow baking dish. Toast at 325 degrees 5-7 minutes, shaking dish until lightly browned and fragrant. Transfer to a plate and cool. Combine walnuts, olives, parsley, green onions, lemon juice and red pepper in a food processor. Pulse until finely chopped. With processor running, slowly add oil until blended. Add Parmesan cheese and pulse a few times.

SERVES 2-4

MARIBEL'S MEXICAN SPAGHETTI

1 package (8 ounce) spaghetti

¼ teaspoon salt

1 can (16 ounce) whole tomatoes

2 garlic cloves, chopped

¼ onion, sliced

4 slices bacon, chopped

1 cup shredded mozzarella cheese

Cook spaghetti in salted water until al dente. Drain and pour in a casserole dish. Combine tomatoes, garlic and onions in a bowl. Mix well. Cook bacon in a skillet until crisp. Add tomato mixture and simmer 5 minutes. Pour mixture over spaghetti. Top with mozzarella cheese. Bake at 350 degrees 20-30 minutes or until cheese melts.

SERVES 4-6

MEAT

Anny's Roast Leg of Lamb

1½ cups tomato juice
¼ cup lemon juice
¼ cup soy sauce
1 tablespoon vegetable or olive oil
2 tablespoons Worcestershire sauce
½ cup chopped red onions

2-3 garlic cloves or 1 teaspoon garlic powder
½ teaspoon chili powder
1 teaspoon salt
1 bay leaf without stem
1 teaspoon sugar

10 sprigs mint
1 lemon, zested
Dash of crushed red pepper
Leg of lamb
Lemon slices
Red wine

Combine tomato juice, lemon juice, soy sauce, oil, Worcestershire sauce, onions, garlic, chili powder, salt, bay leaf, sugar, mint, lemon zest and red pepper in a blender. Process until smooth. Cut fat and fiber from lamb. Place lamb in marinade and marinate 2 hours or overnight. Place in a roasting pan. Heat oven to 450 degrees. Reduce heat and bake at 275-300 degrees 6-8 hours or 30 minutes per pound. Baste with marinade. Place lemon slices on lamb during last 2 hours of baking. Make gravy from pan drippings. Add red wine to deglaze browned bits.

SERVES 10

May substitute 2 tablespoons ketchup and 1 cup hot water for tomato juice.

This recipe was created by Mattie P. Taylor, born July 5, 1868, Taylor Hammond's great, great grandmother and passed down through the generations. A family favorite for Easter. "Anny" was her nickname.

Beef Tenderloin

1 (4 to 5 pound) beef tenderloin

Salt, pepper and lemon pepper to taste

Preheat oven to 500 degrees. Sprinkle tenderloin with salt, pepper and lemon pepper. Place tenderloin on a rack in a shallow roasting pan. Bake 4 minutes per pound. Turn off oven and do not open door. Leave tenderloin in oven 1 hour, 30 minutes or longer for medium doneness. Remove from oven and slice.

SERVES 6-8

May substitute eye of round beef roast for tenderloin.

BEEF STROGANOFF

1 can (6 ounce) sliced mushrooms
  or package sliced mushrooms
1 onion, chopped
4 tablespoons butter

2 pounds sirloin steak, thinly sliced
1 can (15 ounce) beef broth
1 cup sour cream

1-2 tablespoons sherry
Cooked hot rice or noodles

Sauté mushrooms and onions in butter. Remove vegetables from skillet. Brown meat quickly in skillet. Return mushrooms and onions. Add broth. Bring to boil. Blend in sour cream. Cook and stir until thickened. Stir in sherry. Serve over rice or noodles.

SERVES 4

BEEF TACOS

1 tablespoon vegetable oil
1 onion, minced
3 garlic cloves, minced
2 tablespoons chili powder
1 teaspoon ground cumin
1 teaspoon ground coriander

½ teaspoon dried oregano
¼ teaspoon cayenne pepper
1 teaspoon salt
1 pound ground beef
½ cup tomato sauce
½ cup chicken broth

2 teaspoons cider vinegar
1 teaspoon light brown sugar
Salt to taste
8 taco shells
Shredded Cheddar cheese, lettuce,
  tomatoes for garnish

Heat oil in skillet. Sauté onions about 5 minutes until tender. Stir in garlic, chili powder, cumin, coriander, oregano, cayenne and salt. Cook 30 seconds until fragrant. Stir in beef and cook, breaking up until crumbled. Stir in tomato sauce, broth, vinegar and brown sugar. Simmer about 10 minutes until thickened. Add salt. Divide meat filling among taco shells. Serve with shredded Cheddar cheese, lettuce, tomatoes and favorite toppings.

SERVES 4-6

COMPANY MEATLOAF

2 pounds ground chuck
1 small onion, chopped
½ cup breadcrumbs

½ teaspoon pepper
1 can (10¾ ounce) vegetarian
  vegetable soup

1 egg
1 teaspoon salt
Ketchup to taste

Combine meat, onions, breadcrumbs, pepper, soup, egg and salt. Mix well. Shape mixture into a loaf. Place in a 9 x 5-inch loaf pan. Bake at 350-450 degrees 45 minutes. Spread ketchup over top. Bake an additional 15 minutes.

SERVES 8

HH JANELLA BRAND
PRESCHOOL PRINCIPAL

GRILLED BUTTERFLIED LEG OF LAMB

1 cup Dijon mustard
½ cup olive oil
2 tablespoons dry red wine
2 garlic cloves, minced

1 teaspoon dried rosemary
1 teaspoon dried basil
½ teaspoon dried oregano

½ teaspoon dried thyme
¼ teaspoon pepper
1 (4 pound) butterflied leg of lamb

Blend mustard, oil, wine, garlic, rosemary, basil, oregano, thyme and pepper. Add lamb to marinade. Marinate overnight or at least 1 hour at room temperature. Remove from marinade, reserving marinade. Skewer lamb to avoid curling during grilling. Grill over medium coals or to desired degree of doneness. Baste with marinade. Heat remaining marinade and serve with lamb.

SERVES 8

GRILLED MARINATED FLANK STEAK

2 tablespoons lemon juice
2 tablespoons soy sauce
¼ cup olive oil

1 tablespoon dried minced onions
1 teaspoon celery salt

1 teaspoon coarse ground pepper
1½ pound flank steak

Combine lemon juice, soy sauce, oil, onions, celery salt and pepper in a zip-top plastic bag. Mix well. Add steak. Seal bag after getting all air out. Marinate at least 4 hours or overnight. Grill 5 minutes per side for medium rare. Slice diagonally against grain.

SERVES 4

May freeze steak in marinade and thaw when ready to prepare.

GYRO MEATLOAF

1 pound lean ground lamb
1 pound 93% lean ground beef
2 cups fresh breadcrumbs
6 tablespoons minced parsley

1 egg, slightly beaten
1 egg white, slightly beaten
2 large garlic cloves, pressed
2 teaspoons ground cumin

2 teaspoons salt
1 teaspoon pepper or to taste
Tzatziki, p. 118

Break lamb and beef into tablespoon size pieces in a large bowl. Add breadcrumbs, parsley, egg, egg white, garlic, cumin, salt and pepper. Mix well with fork or hands. Shape mixture into a loaf. Place in a greased 9 x 5-inch loaf pan. With a fork or spatula, pull mixture up and away from pan sides. Smooth the top. Bake at 350 degrees 1 hour or until thermometer reaches 150 degrees. Cool to room temperature. Remove from pan. Wrap in plastic wrap and foil. Refrigerate until ready to serve.

SERVES 6

 TZATZIKI

1 English cucumber, shredded
½ cup plain fat free yogurt
1½ cups sour cream

1 small onion, finely chopped
1-3 garlic cloves, pressed
1 tablespoon extra virgin olive oil

1 tablespoon red wine vinegar
Salt and pepper to taste

Place shredded cucumbers in a colander with a dish on top and drain 1 hour. Working in batches, squeeze cucumbers dry. Place in a bowl. Add yogurt, sour cream, onions, garlic, oil, vinegar, salt and pepper. Mix well. Cover and refrigerate 1 hour before serving. Serve cold with gyro meatloaf.

SERVES 3 CUPS

 HAMBURGER STROGANOFF

½ cup finely chopped onions
1 stick butter
1 pound ground sirloin
2 tablespoons all-purpose flour
½-1 teaspoon salt
1½ teaspoons pepper

½ teaspoon garlic powder or
   2 garlic cloves, crushed
1 bay leaf
1 cup sliced mushrooms, fresh or
   canned
1 cup cream chicken soup
⅓ cup red wine (optional)

1 cup sour cream
1 package (3 ounce) cream cheese,
   softened
Cooked egg noodles or noodle of
   choice
Paprika for garnish

Sauté onions in butter until tender. Add beef and cook slowly until browned, crumbling beef. Stir in flour, salt, pepper and garlic until meat is coated and browned. Add bay leaf, mushrooms, soup and wine. Cook 15 minutes. May refrigerate mixture at this point. Reheat mixture thoroughly. Add sour cream and cream cheese just before serving. Stir until smooth. Remove bay leaf. Serve over egg noodles. Top with paprika.

SERVES 4

MARTHA WILLIAM'S
NOT-SO-SLOPPY JOE SQUARES

1¼ pounds ground beef

1 can (8 ounce) tomato sauce

1 package (1½ ounce) Sloppy Joe
   seasoning mix

2 tablespoons chopped onions

½ teaspoon salt

2 packages (8 ounces each)
   refrigerated crescent rolls

1 cup shredded Cheddar cheese

Milk

2 tablespoons sesame seeds

Brown beef in a skillet. Drain well. Stir in tomato sauce, seasoning packet, onions and salt. Mix well. Simmer. Separate each package of rolls into a two large rectangles. Press one dough rectangle in bottom of greased 13 x 9 x 2-inch baking dish, sealing perforations. Spoon hot meat mixture over dough. Sprinkle with Cheddar cheese. Place second dough rectangle over cheese. Brush with milk. Sprinkle with sesame seeds. Bake at 425 degrees 20 minutes or until golden browned. Cool 5-10 minutes. Cut into 10-12 squares.

SERVES 10

Kids love it!

MAMA'S EASY BRISKET

1 bottle (12 ounce) chili sauce

1 package (1 ounce) onion soup mix

¼ cup water (may substitute wine
   or beer)

1 (2-3 pound) beef brisket

Combine chili sauce, onion mix and water. Place brisket in crock pot. Pour mixture over meat. Cook 8-10 hours on low or 6-8 hours on high. Remove from crock pot and cool 20 minutes before cutting.

SERVES 6

Very easy. May combine mixture and brisket and refrigerate overnight.

MEATBALLS

1 pound ground beef
½ cup breadcrumbs
⅓ cup onions (optional)
¼ cup milk

1 egg
1 tablespoon parsley
½ teaspoon Worcestershire sauce

1 jar (10 ounce) grape jelly
1 bottle (12 ounce) chili sauce
1 can (8 ounce) tomato sauce

Combine beef, breadcrumbs, onions, milk, egg, parsley and Worcestershire sauce. Mix well. Shape mixture into 1 inch balls. Brown meatballs in skillet, turning on each side. Drain on paper towels. Melt jelly in saucepan. Add chili sauce and tomato sauce. Mix well. Return meatballs to sauce. Simmer about 20 minutes.

SERVES 4-6

Fabulous with spaghetti.

MEXICALI PIE

1 medium onion, chopped
1 pound ground beef
½ pound sausage
1 can (10¾ ounce) tomato soup

½ small bottle ketchup
1 teaspoon chili powder
1 can (15 ounce) mexicorn with juice

15 sliced green olives
1 package (9 ounce) cornbread muffin mix

Brown onions, beef and sausage. Drain well. Add tomato soup, ketchup, chili powder, mexicorn and green olives. Mix well. Pour mixture into a 11 x 7 x 2-inch baking dish. Cover with foil. Bake at 325 degrees 1 hour. Remove from oven. Prepare cornbread according to package directions. Spread cornbread mixture over meat mixture. Bake at 425 degrees 20 minutes.

SERVES 6

PECAN CRUSTED VENISON
WITH BOURBON MASH

2 cups roasted pecans
½ cup breadcrumbs
2 tablespoons Creole seasoning
12 (3 ounce) venison medallions
Salt and pepper to taste
⅔ cup Creole mustard

6 whole sweet potatoes, skin on
¼ cup heavy cream
¼ cup bourbon
2 tablespoons butter
Salt and pepper to taste
Olive oil

2 tablespoons chopped chives
2 tablespoons finely diced sweet
  red peppers
2 tablespoons finely diced yellow
  peppers

Pulse pecans in food processor until coarsely chopped. Add breadcrumbs and Creole seasoning. Sprinkle each medallion with salt and pepper. Rub Creole mustard over medallions, coating each side completely. Dredge medallions in pecan crumbs, covering completely.

Roast sweet potatoes at 425 degrees 40 minutes. Remove skins and place pulp in saucepan. Mash potatoes over low heat. Stir in cream, bourbon, and butter. Mash until smooth with small lumps. Add salt and pepper. Heat oil in a skillet until smoking hot. Sauté medallions 3 minutes per side for medium rare. To serve, place mashed sweet potatoes under venison and top venison with chives and peppers.

SERVES 4

POT ROAST WITH PORCINI AND BEER

1 (4 pound) beef chuck roast
Coarse salt and pepper to taste
1 tablespoon olive or vegetable oil
1½ pounds thinly sliced onions
2 teaspoons chopped thyme

1 bay leaf
Dash of salt
1 bottle (12 ounce) beer (pale ale)
½ cup water

1 bouillon cube
1 heaping cup dried porcini
  mushrooms
2 tablespoons Dijon mustard

Sprinkle roast with salt and pepper. Cover loosely and refrigerate overnight. If short on time, season at least 1 hour ahead and leave at room temperature. Heat oil in a deep, ovenproof skillet or Dutch oven. Brown meat well until crusty on all sides. Transfer beef to a plate.

Add onions, thyme, bay leaf and salt to pan. Cook, stirring often, until onions are tender and reduced in volume by half. Scrape bottom to use onion juice to release browned bits from beef. Pour in beer and water and crumble in bouillon. Add more pepper to taste. Rinse mushrooms under hot water. Drain, chop and add to pan. Bring to boil. Return beef to sauce. Cover pan and place in a 300 degrees oven. Roast 1 hour. Turn beef over, cover pan and roast an additional 1 hour or until very tender.

Transfer beef to cutting board. Tent with foil and let rest 10 minutes. Tilt pan with towels under one side so sauce gathers on one side. Remove bay leaf. Skim off fat. For thicker sauce, cook over medium heat a few minutes. Stir mustard into sauce. Slice beef and arrange on platter. Drizzle with a little sauce. Serve remaining sauce on the side.

SERVE 6

Porcini mushrooms are only available fresh in the fall. Use dried or substitute morel mushrooms.

PORK TENDERLOIN
WITH MUSTARD SAUCE

¼ cup soy sauce

¼ cup bourbon or apple juice

2 tablespoons brown sugar

1½ pounds pork tenderloin

⅓ cup sour cream

⅓ cup mayonnaise

1 tablespoon dry mustard

1 tablespoon minced onions

1½ teaspoons white vinegar

Blend soy sauce, bourbon and brown sugar in a shallow dish or heavy duty zip-top plastic bag. Pierce pork several times with a fork. Place in marinade. Cover and seal, turning to coat. Let stand 30 minutes at room temperature or refrigerate 8 hours.

Remove pork from marinade and discard marinade. Grill, covered with grill lid, over medium high heat (350-400 degrees) 12 minutes per side or until thermometer reaches 160 degrees. Blend sour cream, mayonnaise, mustard, onions and vinegar. Serve sauce with sliced pork.

SERVES 6

PORK WITH
APPLES, CALVADOS AND CIDER

1½-2 pounds pork tenderloin,
   trimmed and cut into
   1 inch slices
2 tablespoons butter
4 medium golden delicious apples,
   peeled, cored and sliced into
   ⅓ inch slices

1 teaspoon sugar
2 tablespoons butter
Salt and pepper to taste
2 large shallots, finely chopped

1 tablespoon chopped thyme or
   1 teaspoon dried
¼ cup calvados or apple brandy
1 cup whipping cream
¼ cup apple cider

Place pork between plastic wrap. Flatten with a mallet to ¼ inch thickness. May prepare 4 hours in advance and cover and refrigerate. Melt butter in a large skillet. Sauté apples and sugar about 5 minutes until browned. Set aside. Melt butter in a separate skillet. Sprinkle pork with salt and pepper. Brown pork 2 minutes per side, working in batches. Transfer cooked pork to an ovenproof dish. Keep warm in 275 degree oven. Add shallots and thyme to skillet. Sauté 2 minutes. Add calvados and boil gently until reduced to a glaze, scraping up browned bits. Stir in cream and cider. Boil 3 minutes until thickened. Add salt and pepper. Reheat apples. Arrange pork on plates. Spoon sauce over pork and top with apples.

SERVES 4

ROASTED PORK TENDERLOIN
WITH SAGE/CORNBREAD CRUST

1 pound pork tenderloin

2 teaspoons salt

½ teaspoon pepper

1 tablespoon olive oil

1 tablespoon unsalted butter

2 garlic cloves, minced

1 cup crumbled cornbread

1 teaspoon finely chopped sage

Salt and pepper to taste

2 tablespoons Dijon mustard

Pat pork dry and sprinkle with salt and pepper. Heat oil in a 10 inch nonstick skillet until hot. Brown pork, turning, on each side, about 4 minutes. Transfer to an oiled shallow baking pan. Add butter to skillet and sauté garlic about 30 seconds until fragrant. Remove from heat. Stir in cornbread crumbs, sage, salt and pepper. Spread mustard over pork and pat with half seasoned crumbs. Sprinkle with remaining crumbs. Roast at 425 degrees 20-25 minutes until thermometer reaches 155 degrees. If after 25 minutes, crumbs are too brown, tent loosely with foil. Transfer to cutting board, tent with foil and let stand 10 minutes before slicing.

SERVES 4

TEXAS HASH SUPREME

2 pounds ground beef

3 cans (10¾ ounces each) vegetable
   soup, undiluted

Salt and pepper to taste

1 package (8 ounce) shredded extra
   sharp Cheddar cheese

Brown beef and cook until crumbled. Pour off drippings. Add soup. Bring to low boil. Add salt, pepper and Cheddar cheese. Mix until cheese melts.

SERVES 4

H J. RUSSELL FRANK, PH.D
FORMER HIES HEADMASTER

A "Stir by the Fire" delight on any camping trip. This serves 3 campers who have hiked 10 miles carrying 3½ pounds ingredients. Serving will vary, depending upon the exhaustion of the woodland trekkers.

SAUTÉED FILET STEAKS
WITH ROSEMARY AND GREAT HILL BLUE

2 ounces Great Hill Blue cheese or
   other strong cheese
2 tablespoons unsalted butter,
   softened
1 shallot, minced

⅛ teaspoon dry mustard
⅛ teaspoon pepper
4 filet mignon steaks, 1½ inches
   thick tied with butcher's string

Kosher salt and pepper to taste
1½ tablespoons finely chopped
   rosemary
3 tablespoons clarified butter

Cream blue cheese, butter, shallots, mustard and pepper until smooth. Scrape mixture onto a small square of wax paper. Roll mixture up like a sausage, twisting ends. Refrigerate until hard at least 2 hours.

Sprinkle steaks generously with salt and pepper. Top with rosemary. Heat clarified butter over medium heat. Cook steak 5 minutes per side for medium rare. Transfer to plates. Slice cheese roll into quarters. Peel off wax paper. Top each steak with cheese disk. Loosely tent plates with foil 5 minutes. Remove foil and serve.

SERVES 4

ASIAN MARINATED PORK TENDERLOIN

⅓ cup light soy sauce
¼ cup sesame oil
⅓ cup packed light brown sugar

2 tablespoons Worcestershire sauce
2 tablespoons lemon juice
4 garlic cloves, minced

1 tablespoon dry mustard
½ teaspoon pepper
1 pork tenderloin

Blend soy sauce, oil, brown sugar, Worcestershire sauce, lemon juice, garlic, mustard and pepper until smooth. Add pork tenderloin to marinade, turning to coat. Refrigerate 8 hours or overnight. Cook pork to desired degree of doneness.

SERVES 6-8

VENISON STROGANOFF

1¼ cups red wine

3-5 tablespoons Worcestershire sauce

2-4 pound boneless venison roast or whole loin, sliced into ¼-⅓ inch medallions

1 Vidalia or sweet onion, finely chopped

½ bell, sweet red or yellow pepper, thickly sliced

3-5 garlic cloves, minced

Olive oil

½-1 pound mushrooms

Salt or garlic salt, pepper and Worcestershire sauce to taste

1 cup red wine

2-3 tablespoons herbs de Provence

1-2 dashes steak sauce (optional)

1 can (10¾ ounce) cream of mushroom soup

2 tablespoons sour cream

Blend wine and Worcestershire sauce. Add venison medallions. Refrigerate 2-12 hours. Brown onions, peppers and garlic in oil about 3-5 minutes in a large skillet. Add mushrooms and sauté 3-5 minutes until juice forms in skillet. Transfer vegetables and juice to bowl. Add oil to skillet and heat to medium high. Drain meat. Cook venison 6-8 minutes per side until browned. Skim off excess oil. Return vegetables to skillet. Add salt, garlic salt, pepper, Worcestershire sauce, wine and herbs. Cover and cook 1 hour, 30 mintes-2 hours, 30 minutes, stirring occasionally. May add more wine if liquid evaporates. Add 1-2 dashes steak sauce for taste.

Stir in mushroom soup. Cook an additional 20-30 minutes, stirring occasionally. To thin sauce add wine or to thicken, remove cover while cooking. Stir sour cream into sauce or serve as dollop on venison. Serve over white rice, wild, brown rice, potatoes or pasta.

SERVES 6-8

Recommended side dishes are Waldorf salad, early English peas, or French beans and hot buttered biscuits or dinner rolls with Mayhaw jelly and Tupelo honey. Crystal, Texas Pete, Red Rooster or Louisiana Hot Sauce adds spice and nice red color on top of the meat.

Waldorf Salad recipe as follows: Combine 2 red and 2 cubed green apples, handful of red and green seedless grapes, chopped walnuts or pecans and raisins or chopped trail mix. Add some mayonnaise and juice of 1 lemon. Mix well until coated. Add finely chopped celery and sliced maraschino cherries with some cherry juice. Mix well. Refrigerate at least 2 hours. Lightly toss before serving.

This is my "World Famous" venison stroganoff recipe. It works equally well on bucks and does and also various beef and big game cuts (London broil). This dinner will absolutely wow anyone that comes into contact with it and is bullet proof in preparation.

MARINADE FOR
FLANK STEAK OR WILD GAME

1½ cups vegetable oil

¾ cup soy sauce

½ cup Worcestershire sauce

2 tablespoons dry mustard

2½ teaspoons salt

1½ teaspoons dried parsley

1 tablespoon pepper

½ cup red wine vinegar

1 garlic clove, crushed

½ cup lemon juice

Flank steak

Combine oil, soy sauce, Worcestershire sauce, mustard, salt, parsley, pepper, vinegar, garlic and lemon juice in a blender. Process 30-40 seconds. Pour over meat and refrigerate 6-48 hours. Marinate longer for wild game.

SERVES 3 CUPS

MARINADE FOR PORK LOIN

½ cup teriyaki sauce

½ cup soy sauce

3 tablespoons brown sugar

2 green onions, chopped

1 garlic clove, minced

1 tablespoon sesame seeds

½ teaspoon ground ginger

½ teaspoon pepper

1 tablespoon vegetable oil

3 packs pork loins

Blend teriyaki sauce, soy sauce, brown sugar, green onions, garlic, sesame seeds, ginger, pepper and oil until smooth. Enough marinade for 3 packs pork loins. Marinate at least 4 hours. Grill pork over medium coals to desired degree of doneness.

SERVES 15-18

POULTRY

BAKED CHICKEN BREASTS SUPREME

6 boneless skinless chicken breasts
   halves
2 cups sour cream
¼ cup lemon juice
4 teaspoons Worcestershire sauce

4 teaspoons celery salt
2 teaspoon paprika
3 garlic cloves, finely chopped
3 teaspoons salt

½ teaspoon pepper
Dry breadcrumbs
1 stick butter
½ cup vegetable shortening

Rinse chicken breasts and pat dry. Blend sour cream, lemon juice, Worcestershire sauce, celery salt, paprika, garlic, salt and pepper. Add chicken and turn to coat each piece. Cover and refrigerate overnight. Remove chicken from mixture, wiping off excess. Shape chicken by tucking under the ends. Dredge chicken in breadcrumbs, coating evenly. Arrange in a single layer in a large shallow dish. Melt butter and shortening in a small saucepan. Spoon half mixture over chicken. Bake, uncovered, at 350 degrees 45-50 minutes. Pour on remaining butter mixture. Bake an additional 15 minutes or until golden browned.

SERVES 8-12

CHICKEN AND RICE CASSEROLE

3-4 cups cooked and shredded chicken

1 medium onion, diced

1 can (8 ounce) water chestnuts, drained and chopped

2 cans (14½ ounces each) green beans, rinsed and drained

1 can (10¾ ounce) cream of celery soup

1 cup mayonnaise

1 package (6 ounce) long grain wild rice, cooked to package directions

1 cup grated sharp Cheddar cheese

Salt and pepper to taste

Combine chicken, onions, water chestnuts, green beans, soup, mayonnaise, rice, Cheddar cheese, salt and pepper. Pour mixture into a 3 quart casserole dish. Bake at 350 degrees 40 minutes or until bubbly.

SERVES 6-8

CHICKEN ENCHILADAS

4 boneless skinless chicken breasts halves

1 cup sour cream

1 package (12 ounce) shredded Mexican cheese blend

1 can (4 ounce) chopped green chilies

½ cup salsa

1 package (1½ ounce) taco seasoning

1 can (10 ounce) enchilada sauce

1 can (10¾ ounce) cream of chicken soup

1 can (4 ounce) chopped green chilies

Flour tortillas

½ cup shredded sharp Cheddar cheese

Combine chicken, sour cream, Mexican cheese blend, green chilies, salsa and taco seasoning. Blend enchilada sauce, soup and green chilies in a saucepan. Heat until smooth and creamy. Spoon chicken mixture over flour tortillas. Roll up and place in a greased 13 x 9 x 2-inch baking dish. Top with enchilada sauce mixture. Sprinkle with Cheddar cheese. Cover and bake at 350 degrees 15 minutes. Uncover and bake an additional 15 minutes.

SERVES 6-8

CHICKEN MARENGO

2 boneless skinless chicken breast
    halves
Salt and pepper to taste

2 tablespoons unsalted butter
1 onion, finely chopped
2 bacon slices, chopped

⅓ cup dry white wine
1 tablespoon tomato paste
1 cup sliced mushrooms

Pound thickest part of chicken to flatten slightly. Pat dry and sprinkle with salt and pepper. Heat butter in 10 inch skillet over medium high heat until foam subsides. Sauté onions and bacon 2 minutes stirring occasionally. Blend wine and tomato paste. Place onions and bacon to sides of skillet. Add chicken skinned side down and cook 2 minutes until golden browned. Turn chicken and add mushrooms and wine mixture. Mix in onions and bacon. Cover and cook over medium high heat 5 minutes until chicken is done.

SERVES 2

May add black olives also.

CHICKEN POT PIE

3-4 boneless skinless chicken breast
    halves
1 can (10¾ ounce) cream of chicken
    soup
1 cup water

4 chicken bouillon cubes
1 package (10 ounce) frozen mixed
    vegetables, thawed
2 tablespoons butter

½ cup half-and-half
¼ cup all-purpose flour
1 teaspoon salt
2 refrigerated pie pastry sheets

Cook chicken in water until done. Cool and chop. Combine soup, water and bouillon cubes in a separate pan. Bring to boil. Reduce heat and add vegetables and butter. Mix well. Blend half-and-half, flour and salt until smooth. Stir into vegetable mixture. Add chicken. Bring to boil and cook until thickened. Line pie plate with one pastry sheet. Pour chicken mixture over dough. Cover with second pastry sheet. Bake at 400 degrees 30-35 minutes.

SERVES 6-8

CHICKEN PARMESAN

4 boneless skinless chicken breast
   halves
1 large egg, slightly beaten
⅓ cup Italian breadcrumbs

2 tablespoons butter
1¾ cups spaghetti sauce
½ cup shredded mozzarella cheese

2 tablespoons grated Parmesan
   cheese
Angel hair pasta, cooked

Place chicken in a zip-top plastic bag. Flatten with a rolling pin. Dip chicken in egg and dredge in breadcrumbs. Melt butter in a large skillet. Cook chicken 2 minutes per side or until browned. Pour spaghetti sauce over chicken. Cover, reduce heat and simmer 10 minutes. Stir in mozzarella cheese and Parmesan cheese. Simmer 5 minutes or until cheese melts. Serve over angel hair pasta.

SERVES 4

May be prepared in advance. Place in a glass baking dish and cover with foil. Reheat thoroughly.

CHICKEN TETRAZZINI

5 tablespoons butter
½ pound sliced mushrooms
¼ cup chopped onions
¼ cup all-purpose flour
2 cups chicken broth

1¼ cups coffee cream
1 cup grated Cheddar cheese
2 teaspoons salt
⅛ teaspoon pepper

1 teaspoon lemon juice
1 package (8 ounce) angel hair pasta
3 cups cooked chopped chicken
¼ cup grated Parmesan cheese

Melt butter in skillet. Sauté mushrooms and onions. Blend in flour until smooth. Add broth and cream, stirring until smooth and thickened. Stir in Cheddar cheese, salt, pepper and lemon juice until cheese melts. Reduce heat and simmer, uncovered, 10-15 minutes. Cook pasta until al dente. Drain and add to sauce. Stir in chicken. Spoon mixture into a greased 2 quart casserole. Sprinkle with Parmesan cheese. Bake at 400 degrees 20-30 minutes.

SERVES 6

Freezes well.

CHICKEN, SHRIMP, ARTICHOKE CASSEROLE

¾ pound shrimp, peeled and
   deveined
6½ tablespoons butter
4½ tablespoons all-purpose flour
¾ cup whole milk
1 cup heavy cream
1 teaspoon Worcestershire sauce

¼ cup dry sherry
¼ teaspoon salt
¼ teaspoon cayenne pepper
Pepper to taste
1 can (14 ounce) artichokes hearts,
   drained and quartered

2 boneless skinless chicken breast
   halves, cooked and pulled into
   bite size chunks
¼ pound mushrooms, sliced
1 cup grated Parmesan cheese
Paprika for garnish
Hot cooked rice

Cook shrimp until pink. Drain and set aside. Melt butter in a saucepan. Whisk in flour and make a roux. Slowly whisk in milk, then cream, stirring constantly, until thickened. Remove from heat and bring sauce to room temperature. Add Worcestershire sauce, sherry, salt, cayenne and pepper. Mix well. Layer in order artichokes, chicken, shrimp and mushrooms in a greased 11 x 7 x 2-inch baking dish. Sprinkle with Parmesan cheese. Pour white sauce over all. Sprinkle with paprika. Bake at 350 degrees 20-30 minutes or until hot and bubbly. Serve over rice of choice.

SERVES 8

CHICKEN SUPREME

6 boneless skinless chicken breast halves, boiled and cubed

1 package (6 ounce) long grain and wild rice

1 large onion, chopped

1 tablespoon butter

1 can (5 ounce) water chestnuts, drained and sliced

1 can (10¾ ounce) cream of celery soup

1 cup mayonnaise

1 package (10 ounce) frozen French style green beans, thawed, blanched and drained

1 jar (2 ounce) pimentos, sliced and drained

Dash of paprika

Boil chicken in water until done. Drain and tear or cut into bite size pieces. Cook rice according to package directions. Set aside. Sauté onions in butter. Combine chicken, rice, onions, water chestnuts, soup, mayonnaise, green beans and pimentos. Mix well. Spread mixture into a 3 quart glass baking dish. Sprinkle with paprika. Bake at 325 degrees 30-40 minutes until lightly browned.

SERVES 8-10

Great for large gatherings, serve with a salad and bread to make a complete meal.

CHICKEN MARBELLA

4 (2½ pounds) chickens, quartered or all chicken breasts
1 head garlic, peeled and finely puréed
¼ cup dried oregano
Coarse salt and pepper to taste

½ cup red wine vinegar
½ cup olive oil
1 cup pitted prunes
½ cup pitted Spanish green olives
½ cup capers with juice

6 bay leaves
1 cup packed brown sugar
1 cup white wine
¼ cup finely chopped Italian parsley or cilantro

Combine chicken, garlic, oregano, salt, pepper, vinegar, oil, prunes, olives, capers with some juice and bay leaves. Cover and refrigerate overnight. Arrange chicken in a single layer in 1-2 large shallow baking pans. Spoon marinade over top. Sprinkle with brown sugar. Pour wine around chicken. Bake at 350 degrees 50 minutes-1 hour, basting frequently with pan juices. Using a slotted spoon, transfer chicken, prunes, olives and capers to a serving platter. Add a few spoonfuls of pan juices. Top with parsley.

SERVES 15

This is a supper club favorite! Do not let the ingredients turn you off. It is delicious!

CRISPY CHICKEN FINGERS

1 pound boneless skinless chicken breast halves

⅓ cup blue cheese or Caesar dressing

2 teaspoons water

1 teaspoon Tabasco sauce

1 cup crushed cornflakes

1 tablespoon finely chopped parsley

¼ teaspoon salt

Cut chicken into ¾ inch wide and 3 inches long strips. Combine dressing, water and Tabasco in a bowl. Add chicken and stir to coat. Combine cornflakes, parsley and salt. Roll chicken in cornflake mixture to coat. Place chicken strips on foil-lined baking sheet. Freeze 2 hours until firm. Place in a freezer container. May freeze up to 1 month. Place frozen strips in a single layer on a lightly greased baking sheet. Bake at 425 degrees 18-20 minutes. Serve with additional dressing for dipping.

SERVES 6-8

ITALIAN CHICKEN ROLLS

6 boneless skinless chicken breast halves

Dijon mustard

Garlic salt, pepper and Italian seasoning to taste

6 slices mozzarella cheese

All-purpose flour

Salt and pepper to taste

5 tablespoons olive oil

6 green onions, chopped

10-15 mushrooms, sliced

1 cup vermouth or dry white wine

1 can (32 ounce) diced Italian tomatoes with juice

Chopped parsley

Place chicken between two sheets wax paper or plastic wrap. Pound to ¼ inch thickness. Spread mustard over chicken. Sprinkle with garlic salt, pepper and Italian seasoning. Place mozzarella cheese slice over each chicken. Roll up, folding in edges very slightly while rolling. Secure with a toothpick. Combine flour, salt and pepper. Dredge in flour mixture. Heat 3 tablespoons oil in skillet. Sauté chicken until golden browned. Remove from pan and keep warm. Add remaining oil. Sauté green onions 2 minutes. Add mushrooms and sauté 5 minutes more. Stir in wine. Add tomatoes and juice. Simmer until thickened. Stir in parsley. Pour sauce over chicken.

SERVES 6

GRILLED CREOLE MUSTARD MARINATED QUAIL WITH SMOTHERED FIELD PEAS AND ANDOUILLE

QUAIL

½ cup dry white wine
½ cup olive oil
½ cup pure cane syrup
¼ cup Creole or whole grain mustard

½ cup chopped yellow onions
1 tablespoon chopped garlic
½ teaspoon salt
¼ teaspoon pepper

¼ teaspoon cayenne pepper
12 quail (3½ ounces each) breastbones removed and split down the back
2 tablespoons Creole seasoning

FIELD PEAS

1 tablespoon olive oil
2 cups chopped yellow onions
¼ teaspoon pepper
½ pound andouille or fresh pork sausage, remove casing and crumble

2 teaspoons chopped garlic
1 pound dried field peas, picked over and rinsed

1 bay leaf
1 teaspoon thyme leaves
8 cups beef broth

QUAIL

Combine wine, oil, cane syrup, mustard, onions, garlic, salt, pepper and cayenne in a blender. Process 30 seconds until smooth. Sprinkle quail evenly with Creole seasoning. Place in a 2 gallon zip-top plastic bag. Pour in marinade. Seal bag and toss to coat. Refrigerate 12 hours. Remove quail from marinade. Grill about 8 minutes, turning every 2 minutes, until done.

FIELD PEAS

Heat oil in a large heavy stockpot. Sauté onions and pepper 4 minutes until tender and lightly golden browned. Add garlic, peas, bay leaf and thyme. Cook 1 minute, stirring. Add broth and bring to boil. Reduce heat. Cook, uncovered, about 1 hour, 30 minutes until creamy and soft. Remove bay leaf. Keep warm. Mound equal amounts peas on 6 individual plates. Top each with 2 quail.

SERVES 6

MEXICAN CHICKEN TINGA

4 boneless skinless chicken breast
  halves
½ teaspoon salt
1 garlic clove
¼ onion, finely chopped
4-6 medium tomatoes

¼ onion, finely chopped
2 garlic cloves
1 large onion, finely chopped
2 teaspoons vegetable oil
Salt to taste

8 corn tostadas
½ cup sour cream
Shredded lettuce for garnish
¼ cup grated Parmesan cheese

Cook chicken in boiling salted water with garlic and onions until tender. Cool and shred chicken into small pieces. Blend tomatoes, onions and garlic in a food processor. Set aside. Sauté onion in oil until lightly browned. Add tomato mixture. Simmer 5 minutes. Stir in chicken and salt. Cool.

Spread each tostada with sour cream. Top with chicken mixture, lettuce and Parmesan cheese.

SERVES 8

May fold up and serve like tacos.

OVEN FRIED CHICKEN

50 large fryer pieces
1 cup non fat dry milk

¾ quart all-purpose flour
1½ tablespoons salt

5 sticks butter
Paprika for garnish

Rinse and dry chicken. Combine dry milk, flour and salt. Dredge chicken in flour mixture. Place chicken in a single layer on well greased foil-lined baking sheet. Melt butter. Brush butter over chicken. Generously sprinkle paprika over chicken. Bake at 375 degrees about 1 hour or until golden browned.

SERVES 20-25

PINEAPPLE CHICKEN

1½ tablespoons olive oil

1½ cups unbleached or whole wheat flour

¼ teaspoon pepper

1 teaspoon salt (optional)

1½ teaspoons paprika

8 skinless chicken breast or thighs

½ cup chopped bell or sweet red peppers

1 can (20 ounce) pineapple chunks in juice

1 small onion, chopped

¼ cup dry sherry

1 tablespoon brown sugar

Hot cooked brown rice

Heat oil in 13 x 9 x 2-inch baking dish in a 425 degree oven. Combine flour, pepper, salt and paprika in a plastic bag. Shake chicken, one piece at a time, in flour mixture until well coated. When oil is hot, arrange chicken in single layer in pan. Bake 20 minutes, turning chicken. Combine peppers, pineapple, onions, sherry and brown sugar. Pour mixture over chicken. Reduce temperature to 375 degrees. Bake chicken an additional 15-20 minutes until golden browned and sauce thickens. Serve over brown rice.

SERVES 4-6

HH MILLIE TUCKER
PRESCHOOL MUSIC TEACHER

ROAST TURKEY

1 (12 to 16 pound) turkey

Salt and pepper to taste

1 lemon, halved

2 sprigs rosemary

Extra-virgin olive oil

1 tablespoon chopped thyme

Preheat oven to 450 degrees. Place rack in lower third of oven. Remove giblets and neck from turkey, reserving for gravy if desired. Rinse and pat dry. Sprinkle salt and pepper in cavity. Place lemon and rosemary inside. Tuck wing under body. Set on rack, breast side up, in a large roasting pan. Rub with olive oil. Sprinkle with thyme, salt and pepper. Place turkey in oven and lower temperature to 400 degrees. Roast, basting with pan juices, for 2 hours, 30 minutes to 3 hours, 15 minutes or until meat thermometer reaches 165 degrees. Cover with foil to prevent over browning. Let rest, loosely covered with foil, at least 15 minutes before carving.

SERVES 12

PARTY PERFECT CHICKEN

CURRY GLAZE
½ cup chopped onions
6 slices bacon, finely diced
2 tablespoons all-purpose flour
1 tablespoon curry powder

1 tablespoon sugar
1 can (10 ounce) beef consommé
2 tablespoons flaked coconut

2 tablespoons applesauce
2 tablespoons ketchup
2 tablespoons lemon juice

CHICKEN
2 (3 pound) chickens quartered or
   8 chicken breasts

6 tablespoons all-purpose flour
1½ teaspoons salt

1 teaspoon ground ginger
6 tablespoons butter

CURRY GLAZE

Combine onions, bacon, flour, curry, sugar, consommé, coconut, applesauce, ketchup and lemon juice in a saucepan. Mix well. Bring to boil, stirring constantly. Reduce heat and simmer 15 minutes or until thickened.

CHICKEN

Remove skin from chicken. Combine flour, salt and ginger. Shake chicken in flour mixture. Melt butter in large shallow pan. Roll chicken in butter until well coated. Arrange chicken in a single layer in a roasting pan. Bake at 400 degrees 20 minutes. Baste with glaze and bake an additional 20 minutes. Baste with remaining glaze and bake 20 minutes more.

SERVES 8-10

ROSEMARY CHICKEN WITH WHITE WINE

1½ cups all-purpose flour
½ teaspoon garlic powder
6 boneless skinless chicken breasts halves, cubed

2 garlic cloves, minced
3 tablespoons olive oil
1½ cans (15 ounce) chicken broth
1 jar (ounce) capers

½ package sliced mushrooms
1 teaspoon dried rosemary
½-1 cup white wine
Cooked yellow rice

Combine flour and garlic powder. Dredge chicken in flour mixture. Sauté chicken and garlic in hot oil until lightly browned. Add broth, capers, mushrooms, rosemary and wine. Simmer 30-45 minutes, stirring every 5 minutes. Serve over yellow rice.

SERVES 6-7

If sauce thickens, add more chicken broth. May add more garlic salt and white wine or cooking white wine if desired.

Great for a small dinner party.

VIRGINIA'S CHICKEN

1 can (10¾ ounce) cream of celery soup
1 can (10¾ ounce) cream of mushroom soup

½ cup white wine
1 package (8 ounce) shredded mild Cheddar cheese
½ pound mushrooms

6 boneless skinless chicken breast halves
Sliced almonds for garnish

Blend celery soup, mushroom soup, wine, Cheddar cheese and mushrooms. Place chicken in a 13 x 9 x 2-inch baking dish. Pour mixture over chicken. Cover tightly with foil. Bake at 350 degrees 1 hour, 15 minutes. Uncover and sprinkle with almonds. Bake, uncovered, an additional 15 minutes.

SERVES 6

Great with yellow rice and broccoli.

SOUTHWESTERN GRILLED CHICKEN FAJITAS

MARINADE
1 bottle (ounce) Italian dressing

¼ cup lemon juice

⅓-¼ cup Worcestershire sauce

Several dashes Tabasco sauce

CHICKEN
4 boneless skinless chicken breast halves

4 bell pepper or sweet red, yellow or orange, sliced into 10 inch strips

2 sweet onions, sliced into 1 inch strips

Olive oil

3 tablespoons chopped cilantro

4 teaspoons celery salt

4 teaspoons garlic powder

2 teaspoons ground cumin

2-4 teaspoons cayenne pepper

1 dozen flour tortillas

Shredded Cheddar cheese, sour cream, guacamole and salsa for garnish

MARINADE
Blend dressing, lemon juice, Worcestershire sauce and Tabasco.

CHICKEN
Marinate chicken at least 4 hours or overnight. Remove from marinade. Grill 20-25 minutes, turning once. Remove from grill and slice into strips. Place peppers and onions in heavy duty foil. Drizzle liberally with oil. Sprinkle with cilantro, celery salt, garlic powder, cumin and cayenne. Wrap securely in foil. Grill 30 minutes until tender.

Serve chicken and vegetables on separate platters. Fill tortillas as desired. Top with Cheddar cheese, sour cream guacamole or salsa.

SERVES 4-6

TARRAGON CHICKEN BREASTS AND MUSHROOMS

1 tablespoon vegetable oil

6 boneless skinless chicken breast halves

Salt and pepper to taste

1 tablespoon olive oil

½ cup chopped green onions including tops

1 garlic clove, minced

1 package (8 ounce) sliced mushrooms

½ cup rich chicken stock or canned low sodium chicken broth

¼ cup dry white wine

2 tablespoons chopped tarragon or ½ teaspoon dried

⅛ teaspoon white pepper

2 tablespoons all-purpose flour

½ cup sour cream

Heat oil in a skillet. Brown chicken 5 minutes per side. Sprinkle with salt and pepper. Place chicken in a lightly greased 2½ quart casserole dish. Heat oil in skillet. Sauté green onions, garlic and mushrooms 5 minutes until tender. Add to chicken in casserole dish. Add broth, wine, tarragon and pepper to skillet. Stir to blend. Remove from heat. Blend flour and sour cream in a bowl. Whisk into broth mixture. Pour sauce over chicken. Cover and bake at 350 degrees 35-40 minutes until chicken is cooked. Arrange breasts on platter and top with mushrooms and sauce.

SERVES 6

 # SEAFOOD

BASIL-MARINATED SWORDFISH

½ cup olive oil

½ cup vegetable oil

3 tablespoons Dijon mustard

3 tablespoons lemon juice

3 large garlic cloves, minced

1½ cups sliced basil leaves

8 (8 ounces each) swordfish steaks, 1 inch thick

Lemon wedges and basil sprigs for garnish

Whisk together olive oil, vegetable oil, mustard, lemon juice and garlic. Stir in basil. Arrange swordfish steaks in a single layer in a shallow baking dish. Pour marinade over top. Cover and refrigerate 3 hours, turning occasionally. Remove from marinade. Grill 7 minutes per side until cooked through. Place swordfish on plates. Garnish with lemon wedges and basil sprigs.

SERVES 8

FROGMORE STEW

1½ gallons water

1 lemon, juiced

Salt to taste

3 tablespoons Old Bay seasoning or to taste

2 pounds kielbasa sausage, cut into ½ inch pieces

10-12 ears corn on the cob, broken into 3 inch pieces

4 pounds shrimp in shells

Combine water, lemon juice, salt and seasoning in a large stockpot. Bring to boil. Add sausage. Gently boil 5 minutes. Add corn and cook an additional 5 minutes. Begin timing immediately and do not wait for water to return to a boil. Add shrimp and cook 3 minutes more. Remove from heat, drain immediately and serve.

SERVES 8

A classic Low Country recipe can be adjusted to feed a crowd.

BROILED SALMON WITH CHUTNEY AND CRISP SPICED CRUST

SPICED CRUST

3 slices high quality sliced sandwich bread, crust removed

1 cup crushed high quality potato chips

3 tablespoons chopped parsley

2 tablespoons unsalted butter

1 medium garlic clove, minced

½ teaspoon ground cumin

½ teaspoon paprika

¼ teaspoon cinnamon

¼ teaspoon cayenne pepper

¼ teaspoon salt

SALMON

1 salmon fillet

Olive oil

Salt and pepper to taste

1 jar (7 ounce) mango chutney

SPICED CRUST

Pulse bread in a food processor with a steel blade in ¼ inch pieces equaling 1 cup. Spread crumbs evenly over a rimmed baking sheet. Toast 4-5 minutes on lower rack, shaking once or twice, until golden browned and crisp. Combine breadcrumbs, potato chip crumbs and parsley. Set aside.

Heat butter in skillet until melted. Remove from heat. Stir in garlic, cumin, paprika, cinnamon, cayenne and salt. Set butter aside.

SALMON

Coat salmon with oil and sprinkle with salt and pepper. Bake at 350 degrees until done. Remove from oven. Evenly spread 3 tablespoons mango chutney over salmon. Mix butter spice mixture into breadcrumbs. Press breadcrumb mixture onto fish. Return to lower rack. Broil 1 minute until crust is deep golden browned

SERVES 4

This is an excellent company recipe. It is not too difficult if you organize the steps.

CONCH FRITTERS WITH MANGO CHUTNEY

1½ pounds conch meat	3 eggs, beaten	3¼ cups all-purpose flour
2 tablespoons vegetable oil	1½ cups milk	1 tablespoon chopped parsley
½ cup chopped onions	2 teaspoons baking powder	Vegetable shortening
Creole seasoning	1 teaspoon salt	1 cup mango chutney
1 tablespoon chopped garlic	¼ teaspoon cayenne pepper	

Using a meat mallet, pound out conch and dice. Heat oil in skillet. Sauté onions with Creole seasoning 3 minutes until slightly wilted. Sprinkle conch with Creole seasoning. Add conch and sauté 2 minutes. Stir in garlic. Remove and set aside to cool.

Blend eggs, milk, baking powder, salt and cayenne. Add flour, ¼ cup at a time, beating until batter is smooth. Stir in parsley. Fold in conch mixture. Heat shortening to 360 degrees. Drop batter, a heaping tablespoon at a time, into hot oil. When fritters come to surface, roll around with slotted spoon in oil until evenly browned. Transfer to paper towels to drain. Sprinkle with Creole seasoning.

To serve, spoon mango chutney in center of each plate. Arrange fritters around sauce. Garnish with parsley and serve warm.

SERVES ABOUT 2 DOZEN

CRAB CAKES

2 tablespoons unsalted butter
2 tablespoons olive oil
¾ cup small diced red onions
1½ cups small diced celery, about 4 stalks
½ cup small diced sweet red pepper
½ cup small diced yellow pepper
¼ cup minced flat leaf parsley

1 tablespoon capers, drained
¼ teaspoon Tabasco sauce
½ teaspoon Worcestershire sauce
1½ teaspoons Old Bay seasoning
½ teaspoon kosher salt
½ teaspoon pepper
½ pound lump crabmeat, drained and picked over

½ cup plain dry breadcrumbs
½ cup mayonnaise
2 teaspoons Dijon mustard
2 extra large eggs, slightly beaten
4 tablespoons unsalted butter
¼ cup olive oil

Combine butter, oil, red onions, celery, red peppers, yellow peppers, parsley, capers, Tabasco, Worcestershire sauce, Old Bay seasoning, salt and pepper in a large sauté pan. Cook over medium heat 15-20 minutes until soft. Cool to room temperature. Break crabmeat into small pieces in a bowl. Add breadcrumbs, mayonnaise, mustard and eggs. Gently toss to coat. Add vegetable mixture and mix well. Cover and refrigerate 30 minutes. Shape mixture into bite size crab cakes.

Heat butter and oil in a large sauté pan. Cook crab cakes 4-5 minutes per side until browned. Drain on paper towels. Keep warm in a 250 degree oven. Serve hot.

SERVES 26 MINI CRAB CAKES

Crab cakes may be shaped and stored overnight in the refrigerator on baking sheets, covered in plastic wrap. Cook just before serving.

DISHWASHER SALMON FILLETS

SALMON
6 (8-10 ounces each) salmon
   fillets or 6 (10-12 ounce)
   salmon steaks

6 teaspoons butter
Lemon pepper to taste

Garnish with dill sprigs and
   lemon wedges

DILL SAUCE
¼ cup juice from fish
2 tablespoons white wine
½ package Hollandaise sauce mix

1 egg yolk
⅓-½ cup whipping cream
1 tablespoon chopped dill or
   1 teaspoon dried

½ teaspoon lemon pepper
½ teaspoon horseradish (optional)

SALMON

Place salmon on a greased ovenproof plate. Place 1 teaspoon butter on each fillet. Sprinkle with lemon pepper. Place plate on foil and cover fish airtight. Place a large piece foil on top and tuck under to avoid water getting into foil seams. Place in dishwasher on lowest rack. If dishwasher shoots water only in middle, set fish on top rack. Set dishwasher in highest setting. Fish will go through wash-rinse, wash-rinse and hot dry for no longer than 1 hour. Fish is ready. Open foil, drain juice into a bowl. Cover fish with foil and keep warm in oven.

DILL SAUCE

Blend fish juice, wine, Hollandaise sauce mix and egg yolk in a saucepan. Bring to boil, stirring constantly. Stir in cream until smooth. Add dill, lemon pepper and horseradish. Serve sauce with salmon. Garnish salmon with dill sprigs and lemon wedges.

SERVES 6

LIME MARINATED FISH WITH BLACK BEAN SAUCE

3 tablespoons butter, melted
2 limes, juiced
2 tablespoons Creole seasoning (optional)
6 white fish fillets

1 can (16 ounce) black beans, drained
Salt to taste
2 tablespoons sour cream
1 medium ripe tomato, chopped

Salsa of choice
Sour cream and chopped green onions
for garnish
Hot cooked rice

Blend butter, lime juice and seasoning. Marinate fish in butter mixture. Process black beans 5 seconds, just until chopped. Stir in salt and sour cream. Combine tomatoes and salsa. Broil fish until it flakes. Spread a layer of bean sauce on individual plates. Top with fish and salsa mixture. Spoon on sour cream and green onions. Serve with rice

SERVES 6

PACIFIC NORTHWEST SALMON FILLETS

1 stick butter
½ tablespoon honey

½ cup packed brown sugar
2 tablespoons lemon juice

¾ teaspoon crushed red pepper
1 center cut salmon fillet

Combine butter, honey, brown sugar, lemon juice and red pepper in a saucepan. Cook 5-7 minutes over medium heat, stirring until smooth. Cool to room temperature. Arrange salmon in a dish just large enough to hold fish. Pour cooled marinade over fish. Let stand 30 minutes, turning once. Grill 5 minutes per side over medium heat.

SERVES 4

PAELLA

½ cup extra virgin olive oil

4 ounce pork loin, cut into chunks

6 ounces chicken breast, cut into chunks

4 garlic cloves, minced

1 bay leaf

1 onion, julienned

1 bell pepper, cut into strips

1 cup white wine

1 tomato, peeled, seeded and chopped

Dash of saffron

1 teaspoon salt

Pepper to taste

1¼ cups Valencia or short grain rice

2½ cups chicken broth

6 ounces medium shrimp, peeled and deveined

4 ounces scallops

4 ounces squid rings

4 ounces grouper fillet, cut into chunks

6 littleneck clams

6 mussels

¾ cup cooked green peas

6 pimento strips

6 white asparagus spears

1 lemon, wedged

Heat oil in a paella pan. Sauté pork and chicken until golden browned. Add garlic, bay leaf, onions and peppers. Sauté until onions are tender. Add wine, tomatoes, saffron, salt and pepper. Bring to boil. Cook 3 minutes. Add rice and broth. Bring to boil. Add shrimp, scallops, squid, grouper, clams and mussels. Remove from heat. Cover and bake at 350 degrees 20 minutes. Garnish with peas, pimentos, asparagus and lemon wedges.

SERVES 4

This is the same style of Paella served at restaurants on Miami's Calle Ocho.

RED CURRY SHRIMP

1 can (14 ounce) pure coconut milk

½-1 tablespoon red curry paste

1 tablespoon brown sugar

1 pound large shrimp, peeled

2 tablespoons fish sauce

¼ cup chopped basil

Cooked jasmine rice

Heat ½ cup milk in a wok or heavy skillet. Stir in curry paste about 2-3 minutes until blended. Add remaining coconut milk and brown sugar. Bring to boil, stirring constantly. Add shrimp. Reduce heat and simmer 6-8 minutes until shrimp are cooked. Stir in fish sauce and basil. Serve with jasmine rice.

SERVES 4

Add a Mandarin salad for a quick dinner.

POLYNESIAN PRAWNS WITH TROPICAL FRUIT SAUCE

1½ pounds large prawns or shrimp
6 tablespoons rice vinegar
2 tablespoons dark sesame oil

4 teaspoons low sodium soy sauce
1 cup pineapple juice concentrate,
thawed and undiluted

½ teaspoon ground ginger
1 teaspoon minced garlic
2⅔ cups cooked brown rice

Peel and devein prawns, leaving tail. Blend vinegar, oil, soy sauce, pineapple juice, ginger and garlic in a blender. Process until well mixed. Transfer to a large skillet. Bring to boil. Add prawns. Cook, turning frequently, about 2 minutes until opaque. Spoon ⅓ cup hot cooked rice on 8 individual plates. Top each with three prawns and 1 tablespoon sauce.

SERVES 8

This is delicious as well as healthy!

RÉMOULADE SAUCE FOR SHRIMP SALAD

½ cup chopped onions
¾ cup vegetable oil
¼ cup tarragon vinegar
½ cup Creole mustard

2 teaspoons paprika
¾ teaspoon cayenne pepper
2 teaspoons salt
2 medium garlic cloves, chopped

½ cup chopped green onions
2 pounds boiled peeled shrimp
5 cups shredded lettuce

Combine onions, oil, vinegar, mustard, paprika, cayenne, salt and garlic in a blender. Pulse 5 seconds. Pulse another 5 seconds. Add green onions and pulse 2 seconds. Do not blend longer. Place shrimp over lettuce. Pour sauce over shrimp.

SERVES 4-6

SEA SCALLOPS
WITH SAFFRON CHIVE CREAM

12 large sea scallops

½ cup olive oil

Salt and pepper to taste

½ teaspoon saffron

1 cup plus 1 tablespoon sweet vermouth

2 cups heavy cream

1 tablespoon butter

2 tomatoes, peeled, seeded and diced

1 teaspoon finely chopped chives

1 pound baby spinach

1 tablespoon butter

12 asparagus spears, peeled and blanched

Diced tomatoes for garnish

Combine scallops, oil, salt and pepper to a bowl. Marinate. Place saffron and 1 tablespoon vermouth in a small bowl. Allow to steep 10 minutes until liquid turns bright yellow.

Boil 1 cup vermouth in a stainless steel saucepan until reduced by half. Slowly whisk in cream, in a steady stream. Bring to simmer. Add reserved saffron liquid. Cook and stir until sauce coats back of spoon. Remove from heat. Strain sauce into another stainless steel pan. Bring to simmer. Whisk in butter, tomatoes and chives. Remove from heat. Keep cream warm.

Broil scallops 4-5 minutes per side, turning once, until both sides are golden browned. Sauté spinach in skillet with butter until wilted. Divide saffron chive cream among four plates. Place small amount of sautéed spinach in three separate places on plate. Place scallops on each spinach mound. Garnish with asparagus and diced tomatoes. Serve immediately.

SERVES 4

TERIYAKI-GRILLED TUNA

⅔ cup soy sauce

½ cup sherry

1 tablespoon sugar

1 garlic clove, crushed

2 teaspoons finely grated ginger

2 pounds tuna steaks, 2-4 pieces ¾ inch thick

Blend soy sauce, sherry, sugar, garlic and ginger in a saucepan. Bring to boil. Strain into a shallow glass pan. Place tuna in mixture. Marinate about 30 minutes, turning a few times. Grill on a well greased grill 10 minutes per side, basting with marinade.

SERVES 2-4

SHRIMP AND GRITS

GRITS
8 cups water

2 tablespoons butter

1 teaspoon salt

3 cups stone ground grits

½-¾ cup heavy cream

½-1 cup grated Parmesan cheese

SHRIMP
2 tablespoons Emeril's Cajun seasoning

1 tablespoon Italian seasoning

1 tablespoon paprika

2 pounds shrimp, peeled and deveined

4 slices bacon

2 pounds smoked pork sausage

1 tablespoon butter

4 garlic cloves, minced

5 green onions, chopped

1 cup chopped mushrooms or small jar

1 can (14½ ounce) chopped tomatoes

2 tomatoes, peeled and chopped

1 cup chicken broth

2 tablespoons Worcestershire sauce

1 tablespoon Tabasco sauce

½ cup chicken broth

2 tablespoons all-purpose flour

GRITS

Bring water, butter and salt to boil. Stir in grits. Cover, reduce heat and simmer 30 minutes, stirring frequently. Add cream and Parmesan cheese. Stir until heated and creamy. Keep warm.

SHRIMP

Combine Cajun seasoning, Italian seasoning and paprika. Add shrimp and toss to coat. Cook bacon and pork sausage. Remove meat and chop, reserve drippings. Melt butter with drippings. Sauté garlic, green onions and mushrooms until tender. Add canned and fresh tomatoes, 1 cup broth, Worcestershire sauce, Tabasco and shrimp. Cook 2-3 minutes until shrimp are pink. Remove shrimp. Whisk together ½ cup broth and flour. Stir into skillet until thickened. Return shrimp, bacon and sausage. Serve over grits.

SERVES 4-6

SHRIMP CREOLE

¼ cup all-purpose flour
¼ cup bacon drippings
1½ cups chopped onions
1 cup chopped green onions
1 cup chopped celery with leaves
1 cup chopped bell pepper
2 garlic cloves, minced
1 can (6 ounce) tomato paste

1 can (16 ounce) chopped tomatoes
   with juice
1 can (8 ounce) tomato sauce
1 cup water
5 teaspoons salt
1 teaspoon pepper
½ teaspoon crushed red pepper
   (optional)
Tabasco sauce to taste

2-3 bay leaves
1 teaspoon sugar
1 teaspoon Worcestershire sauce
1 tablespoon lemon juice
4 pounds peeled shrimp
½ cup chopped parsley
2-3 cups cooked rice

In a large heavy Dutch oven, blend flour and drippings to make a roux. Add onions, green onions, celery, peppers and garlic. Sauté 20-30 minutes until tender. Stir in tomato paste and mix well. Add tomatoes, tomato sauce, water, salt, pepper, red pepper, Tabasco, bay leaves, sugar, Worcestershire sauce and lemon juice. Cover and simmer 1 hour, stirring occasionally. Add shrimp and cook 5-15 minutes until shrimp turn pink. Allow flavors to blend for awhile. Remove bay leaves. Add parsley before serving. Serve over rice.

SERVES 10

This dish is better made a day in advance. Reheat slowly before serving, do not boil. Freezes well.

SPICY SHRIMP

1¼ pounds raw shrimp, peeled
1 lemon, juiced
2 garlic cloves, minced

½ tablespoon Tabasco sauce
1 teaspoon chili powder
½ teaspoon ground cumin

½ teaspoon salt
1 tablespoon vegetable oil

Combine shrimp, lemon juice, garlic, Tabasco, chili powder, cumin and salt in a bowl. Mix well. Marinate at least 1 hour. Coat baking sheet with oil. Arrange shrimp evenly over sheet. Bake at 425 degrees 12-15 minutes.

SERVES 4

SPICY SHRIMP AND ANDOUILLE OVER CHARLESTON STYLE GRITS

CHARLESTON STYLE GRITS

6 cups water

Salt to taste

1½ cups quick cooking or
    old fashioned grits

2 cups milk

1 cup heavy cream

1 stick butter

Pepper to taste

SHRIMP

2 pounds medium shrimp, peeled
    and deveined

Creole seasoning and salt to taste

8 ounces andouille sausage

1 tablespoon vegetable oil

1 cup finely chopped yellow onions

½ cup finely chopped sweet red
    peppers

½ cup finely chopped bell peppers

2 tablespoons Creole seasoning

1 teaspoon minced garlic

1½ cups low sodium chicken broth

¼ cup heavy cream

2 tablespoons finely chopped green
    onions

2 tablespoons minced parsley

CHARLESTON STYLE GRITS

Bring water to boil in a large stockpot. Add generous amount salt. Stir in grits with wooden spoon. Cook and stir until thickened. Add milk, cream and butter. Return to boil. Cover, reduce heat and simmer 45 minutes-1 hour until smooth and creamy. Sprinkle with salt and pepper. Cover and keep warm.

SHRIMP

Sprinkle shrimp with Creole seasoning and salt. Sauté andouille 3 minutes in a large hot skillet. Transfer to a plate. Add shrimp and cook 2-3 minutes. Remove shrimp to a plate. Heat oil in skillet. Sauté onions and all peppers 3 minutes until tender. Add Creole seasoning. Stir in garlic and cook 1 minute. Add broth. Cook and stir 5 minutes until slightly reduced.

Add cream, green onions and parsley to sauce. Return andouille and shrimp to pan. Bring to simmer. Cook until sauce is slightly reduced. Sprinkle with salt and pepper. Serve over Charleston Style Grits.

SERVES 4-6

❤ YUCATAN MARINATED GROUPER GRILLED IN BANANA LEAVES WITH ORANGE-PINEAPPLE RELISH

ORANGE-PINEAPPLE RELISH

2 limes, juiced
2 tablespoons squeezed orange juice
1 teaspoon chili de arbol powder
2 teaspoons honey

2 tablespoons extra virgin olive oil
½ ripe pineapple, peeled, cored and small diced

2 oranges, peeled and segmented
3 green onions, thinly sliced
3 tablespoons chopped mint
Salt and pepper to taste

GROUPER

4 banana leaves
1½ cups squeezed orange juice
½ cup lime juice
2 tablespoons olive oil

2 tablespoons ancho chili powder
4 teaspoons pasilla chili powder
2 teaspoons chili de arbol powder

4 (8 ounces each) grouper fillets, skinned
Salt and pepper to taste

ORANGE-PINEAPPLE RELISH

Whisk together lime juice, orange juice, chili de arbol, honey and oil. Add pineapple, oranges, green onions, mint, salt and pepper. Mix well. Marinate at least 30 minute at room temperature before serving.

GROUPER

Soak banana leaves in water at least 30 minutes. Whisk together orange juice, lime juice, oil, ancho chili powder, pasilla chili powder and chili de arbol powder. Mix well. Add grouper, turning to coat. Marinate 5 minutes.

Remove banana leaves from water, shaking off excess. Place leaves on a flat surface. Remove grouper from marinade. Sprinkle with salt and pepper. Place 1 fillet on center of leaf. Wrap leaf loosely around fillet. Place packet flat on grill. Close cover and grill 8-10 minutes or until cooked through. Carefully remove from grill. Serve fish in banana leaf with Orange-Pineapple Relish.

SERVES 4

VEGETABLES
AND SIDES

APPLE YAM CASSEROLE

3 sweet potatoes, peeled and cubed
2 Granny Smith apples, peeled,
   cored and sliced
½ cup packed brown sugar

⅓ cup water
¼ teaspoon cinnamon
½ cup raisins
2 tablespoons butter

¼ teaspoon salt
Water
3 tablespoons all-purpose flour
Thin lemon slices

Alternate layers of sweet potatoes and apples in a greased 2 quart casserole dish. Combine brown sugar, water, cinnamon, raisins, butter and salt in a saucepan. Cook over medium heat 5 minutes. Blend small amount of water and flour in a small bowl. Whisk into brown sugar mixture. Pour sauce over sweet potatoes and apples. Place lemon slices on top. Cover and bake at 350 degrees 20 minutes. Uncover and bake an additional 20 minutes until tender.

SERVES 8

Freezes well. Great fall side dish.

ASIAN ASPARAGUS

2 pounds asparagus
¼ cup rice vinegar
¼ cup soy sauce

2 tablespoons vegetable oil
2 teaspoons sugar

1 tablespoon chopped green onions
½ cup chopped pecans

Cook asparagus until crisp-tender. Combine vinegar, soy sauce, oil, sugar and green onions in a zip-top plastic bag. Add asparagus, turning to coat. Refrigerate 3 hours. Transfer to a serving dish. Top with pecans.

SERVES 6

ASPARAGUS CASSEROLE

Buttery round crackers
1 can (12 ounce) cut asparagus

2 hard-cooked eggs, sliced
1 cup white cream sauce

1 tablespoon sliced almonds

Arrange layers of crackers in a buttered casserole dish. Top with layers of asparagus and eggs. Pour on white cream sauce. Sprinkle with almonds. Bake at 350 degrees 15 minutes.

SERVES 2

H JANELLA BRAND
PRESCHOOL PRINCIPAL

CHEESY ZUCCHINI CASSEROLE

6-10 medium zucchini
1 stick butter
¾ cup grated Cheddar cheese
¼ cup grated Swiss cheese

1 container (8 ounce) sour cream
½ teaspoon salt
¼ teaspoon paprika
¼ cup chopped green onions

1 cup breadcrumbs
¼ cup grated Parmesan cheese
Butter

Boil whole zucchini for 10 minutes. Cut ends off, slice lengthwise and arrange in buttered casserole dish. Melt butter and stir in Cheddar cheese, Swiss cheese and sour cream. Add salt, paprika and green onions. Pour sauce over zucchini. Sprinkle breadcrumbs and Parmesan cheese on top. Dot with butter. Bake at 350 degrees 45 minutes.

SERVES 6-8

This cheese sauce would be good on any vegetable.

CHEESE BLITZ CASSEROLE

FILLING

2 packages (8 ounces each) cream
    cheese, softened

1 container (16 ounce) small curd
    cottage cheese

¼ cup sugar

Dash of salt

1 lemon, juiced

BATTER

2 sticks butter, melted

½ cup sugar

2 eggs

1 cup sifted flour

3 teaspoons baking powder

Dash of salt

¼ cup milk

1 teaspoon vanilla

FILLING

Blend cream cheese, cottage cheese, sugar, salt and lemon juice until smooth.

BATTER

Combine butter, sugar, eggs, flour, baking powder, salt, milk and vanilla. Mix well until smooth. Pour half batter into bottom of greased 13 x 9 x 2-inch baking dish. Spread filling over batter, covering to edges. Top with remaining batter. Bake at 300 degrees 45 minutes or until set and golden browned.

SERVES 10-12

May be served with sour cream or lemon yogurt. Great with sausage and egg casserole for brunch.

I brought this dish to a HIES mom's brunch years ago before I knew anyone and so many asked me for the recipe it has been floating around HIES ever since!

CLASSIC MEXICAN FRIED BEANS WITH ONIONS AND GARLIC

2 tablespoons vegetable oil
1 medium white onion, chopped
4 garlic cloves, peeled and finely chopped

4 cups seasoned cooked beans, slightly warm
Salt to taste

½ cup crumbled Mexican queso fresco, queso anejo, pressed, salted farmers cheese, dry feta or Parmesan cheese for garnish
Tortilla chips

Heat oil in a well seasoned or nonstick skillet over medium heat. Sauté onions, 10 minutes, stirring frequently, until deep golden browned. Add garlic and cook 1 minute. Using a slotted spoon, scoop in about ¼ beans, leaving liquid behind. Mash beans into a coarse purée. Add another portion of beans. Mash until puréed. Continue adding beans until all beans are mashed.

Add 1 cup bean liquid, stir frequently, until thickened. Top with cheese of choice and tortilla chips.

SERVES 6

CREAM CHEESE MASHED POTATOES

5 pounds baking potatoes, peeled and cubed
2 packages (3 ounces each) cream cheese, softened

1 container (8 ounce) sour cream
½ cup milk
2 teaspoons onion salt

Paprika or chopped parsley for garnish

Cook potatoes in boiling water 15-20 minutes or until tender. Drain and place in large bowl. Add cream cheese, sour cream, milk and onion salt. Beat at medium speed with electric mixer until smooth and fluffy. Do not over beat. Spoon into a lightly greased 13 x 9 x 2-inch or 3 quart baking dish. Cover and bake at 325 degrees 50 minutes until thoroughly heated. Top with paprika or parsley.

SERVES 10

Unbaked mashed potatoes may be refrigerated up to 2 days. Let stand at room temperature 30 minutes and bake as directed.

Cranberry Sauce

1 cup water

1 cup sugar

1 cinnamon stick

2 teaspoons finely chopped ginger

2 teaspoons orange zest

¼ teaspoon salt

⅛ teaspoon ground cloves

1 package (12 ounce) fresh cranberries

Combine water, sugar, cinnamon stick, ginger, orange zest, salt and cloves in a medium saucepan. Cook over medium heat, stirring constantly, until sugar dissolves. Stir in cranberries. Bring to boil. Reduce heat and simmer about 8 minutes, stirring until slightly thickened. Transfer to a serving bowl. Remove cinnamon stick. Cool.

SERVES 6

 # Ginger Carrots

3 medium carrots, peeled and cut into 3¼ inch long slices

1 tablespoon margarine

1 tablespoon brown sugar

⅛ teaspoon ground ginger

Cook carrots in small amount boiling water until crisp-tender. Drain and set aside. Melt margarine in saucepan. Stir in brown sugar and ginger. Cook over medium low heat, stirring constantly, until sugar dissolves. Add carrots and stir until coated. Heat thoroughly.

SERVES 2

ENDIVE GRATIN

6 large endives outer leaves removed

4 cups chicken broth

1 lemon, juiced

1 teaspoon salt

2 slices bacon, cut into ½ inch pieces

1½ cups grated Tomme de Savoie cheese

1½ cups grated Gruyère cheese

Arrange endive in a single layer in a deep skillet. Add broth, lemon juice and salt. Cover with round piece of parchment paper. Make a small hole in center of paper. Bring to boil. Reduce heat and simmer 30 minutes, turning occasionally, until endives are tender. Remove endive and pat dry.

Cook bacon in same skillet 3 minutes until lightly browned. Add endive and reduce heat. Cook 10 minutes, turning occasionally until evenly browned. Transfer endive and bacon to a gratin dish. Sprinkle with Tomme de Savoie and Gruyère cheese. Broil about 5 minutes, turning dish until cheese is evenly browned. Serve immediately.

SERVES 6

May be made in advance through the browning and refrigerated overnight. Reheat endives before proceeding.

♡ GREEN BEANS VINAIGRETTE

2 pounds green beans
½ cup olive oil

2 teaspoons lemon zest strips or zest
2 garlic cloves, minced

½ teaspoon salt
¼ teaspoon crushed red pepper

Cook beans in boiling water 12-15 minutes until tender. Drain and cool. Combine oil, lemon strips, garlic, salt and red pepper in a jar. Cover tightly and shake well. Place beans in a large plastic bag. Add oil mixture, seal and turn to coat. Refrigerate 2 hours. Turn occasionally.

SERVES 6-8

GREEN BEANS WITH TOMATO AND FRESH BASIL

1½ pounds green beans,
    rinsed and trimmed
4 tablespoons butter
½ tablespoon sugar

¾ teaspoon garlic salt
⅛ teaspoon salt
⅛ teaspoon pepper

½ bag chopped basil
2 cups cherry or grape tomatoes,
    halved

Cook green beans in boiling water 5 minutes. Drain and plunge into cold water. Drain again. Melt butter in a skillet. Stir in green beans, sugar, garlic salt, salt, pepper and basil. Cook 5 minutes. Add tomatoes and cook 3-5 minutes until tender but not mushy.

SERVE 4

This is a family favorite. Very easy and very tasty.

HASH BROWN CASSEROLE

2 pounds shredded hash brown
potatoes
4 tablespoons butter, softened
1-2 cups sour cream

1 package (8 ounce) shredded sharp
Cheddar cheese
½-¾ cup sautéed chopped onions
1 can (10¾ ounce) cream of chicken
soup

1 teaspoon salt
1 cup cornflakes cereal (optional)
2 tablespoons butter (optional)

Combine potatoes, butter, sour cream, Cheddar cheese, onions, soup and salt. Mix well. Spoon mixture into a casserole dish. Top with cornflakes. Dot with butter. Bake at 350 degrees 55 minutes.

SERVES 8-10

OVEN FRIES

2½ pounds baking potatoes,
scrubbed and cut into ½ inch
thick fries

1 teaspoon vegetable oil
1 tablespoon sugar

1 teaspoon salt
Pinch of cayenne pepper

Preheat oven to 450 degrees. Combine potatoes, oil, sugar, salt and cayenne in a large bowl. Mix until well coated. Spread potatoes out in a single layer onto a foil-lined greased baking sheet. Bake 30 minutes until tender and browned. Serve immediately.

SERVES 4-6

MEXICAN RICE

2 tomatoes
½ cup water
1 garlic clove

3 onion slices
1 cup white rice
1 tablespoon vegetable oil

3 cups chicken broth
½ cup canned mixed vegetables

Blend tomatoes, water, garlic and onions in food processor. Cook rice in oil in a skillet until lightly browned. Add tomato mixture. Cook over medium-low heat 2 minutes. Add broth and vegetables. Simmer 20 minutes.

SERVES 4-6

MUSHROOMS IN SOUR CREAM

1 ¼ pounds mushrooms
½ lemon, juiced
Salt and white pepper to taste

1 medium onion, halved and thinly
  sliced
1 tablespoon white wine vinegar
½ teaspoon sugar

1 cup sour cream
¼ teaspoon Tabasco sauce
1-2 tablespoons Dijon mustard
Paprika for garnish

Clean mushrooms. Slice off bottom of stem. Combine mushrooms, lemon juice, salt and pepper in a saucepan. Cover tightly and bring to boil. Cook, shaking pan to toss mushrooms, about 4 minutes. Uncover and cook over high heat until reduced to 2-3 tablespoons liquid and 2 cups cooked mushrooms. Refrigerate.

Pour boiling water over onions, drain immediately and run under cold water. Drain well. Blend vinegar, sugar, salt, onions, sour cream, pepper, Tabasco and mustard in a bowl. Mix well. Stir in cold mushrooms. Spoon into a serving bowl. Top with paprika. Refrigerate until ready to serve.

SERVES 6-8

POPEYE'S RISOTTO

2 garlic cloves, minced
2 tablespoons olive oil
2 tablespoons butter

1 cup Arborio rice
4 cups chicken broth
1 bag baby spinach

Salt and pepper to taste
Grated Parmesan cheese

Sauté garlic in oil and butter. Add rice, toss to coat and cook 3 minutes. Add 2 cups broth, one cup at a time, stirring constantly. After first cup is absorbed, add second cup. Place 2 cups broth in a blender. Gradually blend in spinach. After second cup of broth, begin adding spinach broth, one cup at a time, until rice is tender. Stir in salt and pepper. Top with Parmesan cheese.

SERVES 8

May add ½ cup wine or add ½ cup Parmesan cheese with final cup of broth. May substitute ½ cup half-and-half or milk for ½ cup broth.

 KIRK AND LIZZIE DUNCAN
CURRENT HEADMASTER

POTATO CASSEROLE

1 package (2 pound) hash browns
4 tablespoons butter, melted
1 container (8 ounce) sour cream
1 teaspoon pepper

1 can (10¾ ounce) cream of chicken soup
½ cup chopped onion
1 package (8 ounce) shredded sharp Cheddar cheese

Breadcrumbs
4 tablespoons butter, melted
Toasted almonds for garnish

Combine hash browns and butter. In a separate bowl, blend sour cream, pepper, soup, onions and 1½ cups Cheddar cheese. Add mixture to potatoes and mix well. Pour mixture into a 3 quart glass dish. Top with breadcrumbs. Drizzle with butter. Top with almonds and remaining ½ cup Cheddar cheese. Bake at 350 degrees 50 minutes to 1 hour.

SERVES 8-10

May be prepared a day in advance and baked the next day. Mixture does not need salt because of the soup.

Roasted Asparagus

1 bunch asparagus, trimmed

1 sweet red pepper, cut into strips

2 tablespoons butter, melted

2 tablespoons olive oil

Chopped parsley, salt and pepper
to taste

Layer asparagus and peppers in a casserole dish. Blend butter and oil. Drizzle over vegetables. Sprinkle with parsley, salt and pepper. Cover with foil. Bake at 350 degrees 30 minutes.

Serves 4

The red and green colors look pretty for Christmas. Substitute yellow peppers in spring.

❤ Roasted Winter Vegetables

1 pound carrots, peeled and cut
into 1¼ inch cubes

1 pound parsnips, peeled and cut
into 1¼ inch cubes

1 large sweet potato, peeled and
cut into 1¼ inch cubes

1 small butternut squash, peeled,
seeded and cut into 1¼ inch
cubes

3 teaspoons quality olive oil

1½ teaspoons kosher salt

½ teaspoon pepper

2 teaspoons chopped Italian parsley

Place carrots, parsnips, potatoes and squash in a single layer on two baking sheets. Drizzle with oil. Sprinkle with salt and pepper. Toss well. Bake at 425 degrees 25-35 minutes until all vegetables are tender, turning once with metal spatula. Sprinkle with parsley. Add more salt and pepper if desired.

Serves 8

These vegetables also make a delicious soup. Purée one batch of roasted vegetables with 6-8 cups hot chicken broth. You have Roasted Vegetable Soup.

ROSIE'S VIDALIA ONION PIE

1 (9 inch) pie crust, unbaked

Egg white

2 pounds or 3-4 medium Vidalia
    sweet onions

1 stick butter

3 eggs, beaten

1 cup low fat sour cream

¼ teaspoon salt

½ teaspoon white pepper

¼ teaspoon cayenne pepper or
    dash of Tabasco sauce

½ cup grated Parmesan cheese

Brush pie crust with egg white. Bake at 350 degrees about 2 minutes until dull in color. Thinly slice onions and then quarter. Sauté onions in butter. Combine eggs, sour cream, salt, pepper and cayenne. Mix until smooth. Spoon onions into crust. Pour egg mixture over top. Sprinkle with Parmesan cheese. Bake at 450 degrees 15-20 minutes. Reduce heat to 325 degrees and bake 15-20 minutes or until lightly browned.

SERVES 6

SOUTHERN COOKED GREENS

½ pound bacon

3 cups julienned onions

Salt and pepper to taste

Dash of cayenne pepper

2 tablespoons minced shallots

1 tablespoon minced garlic

1 bottle (12 ounce) Dixie beer

¼ cup rice wine vinegar

1 tablespoon molasses

6 pounds mustard greens or collard
    greens, turnip greens, kale or
    spinach, rinsed and stemmed

Cook bacon 5 minutes in a large stockpot until crispy. Add onions and cook about 6-7 minutes until wilted. Add salt, pepper and cayenne. Stir in shallots and garlic and cook 2 minutes.

Pour in beer, vinegar and molasses. Stir in greens, one-third at a time, pressing down when wilted. Cook, uncovered, about 1 hour, 15 minutes. Mound greens in center of platter. May arrange pork chops around greens and cover with sauce.

SERVES 8

SAVOY CABBAGE
WITH PANCETTA AND GORGONZOLA

DRESSING

4 teaspoons white vinegar

1 tablespoon Dijon mustard

2 garlic cloves, minced

⅓ cup olive oil

CABBAGE

1 tablespoon olive oil

¼ pound pancetta, cut into ⅛ inch dice

1 small head Savoy cabbage, quartered, cored and very thinly sliced

½ teaspoon cracked pepper

¼ pound Gorgonzola cheese, crumbled

DRESSING

Combine vinegar, mustard and garlic in a food processor. Process until creamy. With machine running, add oil in a steady stream. Set aside.

CABBAGE

Heat oil in a skillet over medium high heat. Cook pancetta until crisp but not dark browned. Remove pancetta and all but 3 tablespoons drippings. Transfer drippings to a large skillet and heat. Add cabbage and cook 2-3 minutes until wilted. Add reserved pancetta, pepper and dressing. Toss to coat. Cook 1 minute. Add half Gorgonzola cheese. Cook until cheese begins to melt. Divide cabbage among four plates. Sprinkle with remaining Gorgonzola cheese and serve immediately.

SERVES 4

Spinach Artichoke Casserole

1 package (30 ounce) frozen chopped spinach, thawed
1 small onion, minced
1 stick margarine, melted
½ cup sour cream

1 package (8 ounce) cream cheese, softened
1 teaspoon lemon juice
½ teaspoon garlic salt

⅓ cup grated Parmesan cheese
1 jar (14 ounce) marinated artichokes
1 cup saltine cracker crumbs

Cook spinach according to package directions. Drain and reserve ¼ cup spinach juice. Sauté onions in margarine in a large skillet. Add sour cream, cream cheese, lemon juice, garlic salt, Parmesan cheese and reserved spinach juice. Mix well. Add spinach and mix until well blended. Cut artichokes into bite size pieces. Place artichokes in bottom of a 13 x 9 x 2-inch baking dish. Pour spinach mixture over top. Sprinkle with cracker crumbs. Drizzle with margarine. Bake at 350 degrees 30-45 minutes.

Serve 8-10

♡ Tuscany Green Beans

1 garlic clove, minced
3 tablespoons olive oil

1 cup seeded and finely chopped tomatoes
2 tablespoons red wine vinegar

1 teaspoon dried oregano
Salt and pepper to taste
1 pound green beans

Cook garlic in oil in saucepan until golden browned. Add tomatoes, vinegar, oregano, salt and pepper. Stir until warm and blended. Remove from heat. Cover and keep warm.

Boil or steam green beans until crisp-tender. Drain well. Place beans on a warm serving platter. Spoon warm sauce over green beans.

Serves 6

SPINACH AND ARTICHOKE IN PUFF PASTRY

1 package (10 ounce) frozen
  chopped spinach, thawed
1 can (14 ounce) artichokes hearts,
  drained and chopped

½ cup mayonnaise
½ cup grated Parmesan cheese
1 teaspoon onion powder
1 teaspoon garlic powder

½ teaspoon pepper
1 package (17 ounce) frozen puff
  pastry, thawed for 30 minutes

Drain spinach well, pressing between layers of paper towels. Combine spinach, artichokes, mayonnaise, Parmesan cheese, onion powder, garlic powder and pepper. Mix well.

Thaw puff pastry at room temperature 30 minutes. Unfold pastry and place on a lightly floured surface or heavy duty plastic wrap. Spread ¼ spinach evenly over pastry sheet, leaving ½ inch border. Roll up jelly roll fashion, pressing to seal seams. Wrap in heavy duty plastic wrap. Repeat with remaining pastry and spinach mixture. Freeze 30 minutes.

Cut rolls into ½ inch thick slices. Bake at 400 degrees 20 minutes or until golden browned.

SERVES 4 DOZEN

Rolls may be frozen for up to 3 months.

SPINACH MADELINE

2 packages (10 ounces each) frozen
    chopped spinach, thawed
4 tablespoons butter
2 tablespoons all-purpose flour
2 tablespoons minced onions

½ teaspoon pepper
1 teaspoon Worcestershire sauce
¾ teaspoon celery salt
⅓ teaspoon salt
¾ teaspoon garlic salt

1 package (8 ounce) Mexican
    processed cheese loaf, cubed
1 sleeve saltine crackers, crushed
Paprika for garnish

Cook spinach according to package directions. Drain and reserve ½ cup juice. Melt butter in a large saucepan. Stir in flour and onions. Add spinach juice, stirring until smooth. Add pepper, Worcestershire sauce, celery salt, salt, garlic salt and Mexican cheese. Cook and stir until cheese melts. Stir spinach into cheese mixture. Pour mixture into a shallow 1 quart baking dish. Cover with cracker crumbs. Lightly sprinkle with paprika. Bake at 350 degrees 30 minutes.

SERVES 10

This is a wonderful side dish for a buffet. It compliments all types of meat entrées. It is a real crowd pleaser and can be made a day in advance and refrigerated until baked. Spinach Madeline is always served at my family Thanksgiving and Christmas Eve dinners.

SQUASH CASSEROLE

6 cups large diced yellow squash
    and zucchini
Vegetable oil
1 large onion, chopped
4 tablespoons butter

½ cup sour cream
⅔ teaspoon salt
⅙ teaspoon pepper
⅙ teaspoon garlic powder

1 cup grated Cheddar cheese
1 cup crushed buttery round
    crackers

Sauté squash in oil over medium heat 15-20 minutes until completely broken down. Line a colander with clean towel. Place cooked squash in lined colander. Squeeze excess moisture from squash. Set aside.

Sauté onions in butter 5 minutes in a skillet. Combine onions, squash, sour cream, salt, pepper, garlic powder and Cheddar cheese. Mix well. Pour mixture into a buttered casserole dish. Top with cracker crumbs. Bake at 350 degrees 25-30 minutes.

SERVES 6

TOMATO AND ONION TART

2 large onions (1½ pounds), thinly sliced

2 tablespoons olive oil

Pastry dough for 12 inch single tart crust

2 cups shredded Monterey Jack or Gruyère cheese

½ pound plum tomatoes, thinly sliced

¼ cup Niçoise olives, pitted

Salt and pepper to taste

Cover and cook onions in oil 20 minutes in a large skillet, stirring occasionally until tender. Remove lid and cook onions, stirring occasionally, until golden browned and liquid evaporates. Remove from heat and cool onions slightly.

Press pastry dough into a 12 inch tart pan or quiche dish. Spread onion mixture over dough and top with Jack cheese. Arrange tomatoes in circles over cheese. Top with olives. Sprinkle with salt and pepper. Bake at 375 degrees 45 minutes or until golden browned. Cool on rack. Serve warm or at room temperature.

SERVES 10

TWICE BAKED POTATOES

4 large baking potatoes

4-5 tablespoons margarine or butter

Salt and pepper to taste

2 tablespoons chopped chives

1 cup milk

Grated Cheddar cheese

Rinse and pierce potatoes with a fork. Bake at 375 degrees about 1 hour. While hot, carefully cut potato in half, so as to not tear outside. Scoop out pulp with a spoon and place in a bowl. Leave some pulp in skins. Mash potato pulp well with potato masher. Add butter and mash again. Add salt, pepper and chives. Slowly whip in milk until soft and fluffy but not runny. Spoon potato mixture back into skins until even with skin edge. Cover generously with Cheddar cheese. Bake at 350 degrees 25-30 minutes.

SERVES 8

May also add sour cream in place of some milk. Top with cooked and crumbled bacon, chopped parsley or minced onions, if desired.

SWEET POTATO SOUFFLÉ

SWEET POTATOES

3 cups cooked peeled and mashed
sweet potatoes

2 eggs, well beaten

1 cup packed brown sugar or
granulated sugar

½ cup milk

1 teaspoon vanilla

5⅓ tablespoons butter, melted

TOPPING

1 cup packed brown sugar

1 cup chopped nuts

⅓ cup all-purpose flour

5⅓ tablespoons butter, melted

SWEET POTATOES

Combine sweet potatoes, eggs, brown sugar, milk, vanilla and butter. Mix well. Pour mixture into a greased 13 x 9 x 2-inch baking dish.

TOPPING

Blend brown sugar, nuts, flour and butter. Mix well. Sprinkle over sweet potatoes. Bake at 350 degrees 25-30 minutes.

SERVES 8-10

Yummy Veggie Kabobs

10 medium shiitake mushrooms

½ medium sweet red pepper, cut into 1½ inch pieces

½ bell pepper, cut into 1½ inch pieces

1 medium yellow onion, cut into 1½ inch pieces

2 teaspoons olive oil

1 teaspoon dried thyme

1 teaspoon dried dill

½ teaspoon salt

10 bamboo sticks or skewers

Combine mushrooms, sweet red peppers, bell peppers and onions in a large bowl. Add olive oil, thyme and dill. Stir until well coated. Loosely skewer vegetable pieces of uniform size. Do not overload skewers. Refrigerate at least 1 hour. Grill about 10-15 minutes, turning frequently.

SERVES 5

May add other vegetables such as zucchini, eggplant or chilies.

DESSERTS

BLACK BOTTOM PIE

4 egg yolks, beaten
2 cups milk, scalded
3 tablespoons all-purpose flour
½ cup sugar
1½ semi-sweet chocolate baking
   squares, grated

1 tablespoon vanilla
1 (10 inch) pie crust, baked
1 tablespoon gelatin
¼ cup cold water
¼ teaspoon cream of tartar
4 egg whites, stiffly beaten

½ cup sugar
1 tablespoon rum extract
1 cup heavy cream, whipped
½ semi-sweet chocolate baking
   square, grated

Slowly add egg yolks to scalded milk. Combine flour and sugar. Add to milk mixture. Cook 5 minutes, stirring constantly, or until mixture coats back of spoon. Remove from heat. Measure out 1 cup custard and add to 1½ grated chocolate squares. Stir in vanilla. Mix well. Cool and pour into pie crust. Refrigerate.

Dissolve gelatin in cold water. Stir into remaining hot custard. Cool. Beat cream of tartar into egg whites until stiff. Gradually beat in sugar. Fold into custard. Stir in rum extract. Pour custard over cold chocolate custard. Refrigerate until firm. Spread whipped cream over top. Sprinkle with grated chocolate.

SERVES 8

This takes a little time, but is delicious and very pretty.

This is an old recipe that belonged to my grandmother and then my mother. About 40 years ago, I entered it in a baking contest at the old downtown Davison's Department Store on Peachtree Street (later Macy's). It won second prize.

BLACK BOTTOM PEANUT BUTTER MOUSSE PIE

CRUST
7 whole graham crackers, broken | 4 tablespoons butter, melted | 2 tablespoons sugar

CHOCOLATE FILLING
1⅓ cups semi-sweet chocolate chips | 2 tablespoons light corn syrup | 1 teaspoon vanilla
⅔ cup heavy cream

PEANUT BUTTER MOUSSE
1 cup peanut butter chips | 1 teaspoon vanilla | 1 teaspoon vanilla
¾ cup heavy cream | 1 cup heavy cream | 2 tablespoons sugar
3 tablespoons peanut butter

CRUST

Blend crackers, butter and sugar in a food processor until crumbly. Press into bottom and up sides of 9 inch pie plate.

CHOCOLATE FILLING

Microwave chocolate chips and cream about 3 minutes until softened. Whisk in corn syrup and vanilla until smooth. Spread over crust. Freeze about 10 minutes.

PEANUT BUTTER MOUSSE

Microwave peanut butter chips and cream until softened. Whisk in peanut butter and vanilla. Beat 1 cup cream, vanilla and sugar until thickened but no peaks. Fold into peanut butter mixture. Spoon mousse over chocolate layer. Refrigerate 1 hour or up to 1 day.

SERVES 8

BANANA PUDDING

¾ cup sugar

2 tablespoons cornstarch

3 cups milk

4 egg yolks, slightly beaten

1 teaspoon vanilla

4 tablespoons butter

3 medium bananas, sliced

1 package (12 ounce) vanilla wafers

3 eggs whites (optional)

¼ teaspoon cream of tartar
  (optional)

¼ cup sugar (optional)

Combine sugar and cornstarch in top of double boiler. Slowly add milk. Cook and stir until thickened. Add small pudding to egg yolks. Mix well. Stir egg mixture into pudding. Cook 2 minutes. Remove from heat. Add vanilla and butter. Cool. Alternate layers of pudding, bananas and wafers, beginning and ending with pudding, in a 9 x 9-inch baking dish.

Beat egg whites and cream of tartar until soft peaks form. Gradually beat in sugar until stiff peaks form. Spread topping over pudding. Bake until meringue is golden browned.

SERVES 6-8

CHOCOLATE PEANUT BUTTER BARS

1 jar (18 ounce) creamy peanut
  butter

3 cups sugar

1 cup light corn syrup

½ cup water

½ pound milk chocolate, melted

Place peanut butter in a large greased bowl. Melt sugar, corn syrup and water in a saucepan. Cook and stir until sugar dissolves. Bring to boil. Cook and stir until temperature reaches 290 degrees. Pour syrup over peanut butter and stir quickly. Pour mixture onto a buttered baking sheet. Cover with wax paper. Cool slightly. Cut into squares while still warm. Spread chocolate over bars.

SERVES 10-12

BREAD PUDDING

PUDDING

4 cups heavy cream

1 pound French bread, torn into
  1 inch pieces

3 eggs, slightly beaten

2 cups sugar

2 tablespoons vanilla

1 package (12 ounce) white
  chocolate chips

SAUCE

1 package (12 ounce) white
  chocolate chips

1 cup heavy cream

PUDDING

Pour cream over bread. Soak about 5 minutes. Stir in eggs, sugar and vanilla. Add white chocolate chips. Pour mixture into a greased 13 x 9 x 2-inch baking dish. Bake at 350 degrees 1 hour.

SAUCE

Combine white chocolate chips and cream in a glass bowl. Microwave until chocolate melts and is smooth, stirring every minute. Spoon sauce over pudding and serve immediately.

SERVES 8-10

DESSERTS

CHOCOLATE TOFFEE BARS

1 stick butter, melted
1¾ cups crushed chocolate grahams crackers or wafer cookies
1¼ cups almond brickle chips
1 package (12 ounce) mini toffee bars, crushed
1 cup semi-sweet chocolate chips
1 cup chopped pecans
½ cup chopped walnuts
1 can (14 ounce) sweetened condensed milk

Line a 13 x 9 x 2-inch baking dish with foil, extending over ends. Pour butter into pan. Sprinkle cracker crumbs over butter. Press firmly into a crust. Bake at 350 degrees 5 minutes.

Layer in order brickle chips, toffee crumbs, chocolate chips, pecans and walnuts over crust. Press layers down firmly. Pour milk over all. Bake at 325 degrees 30 minutes or until edges are lightly browned. Cool completely in pan. Lift foil out of pan. Cut into bars.

SERVES 2 DOZEN

May make in advance and freeze. Great to make for gifts.

CUSTARD PERFECTO

2-3 eggs
½ cup sugar
⅛ teaspoon salt
1 teaspoon vanilla
2 cups whole milk, warm
Ground nutmeg

Beat eggs with a wire whisk. Stir in sugar, salt and vanilla. Add warm milk and mix well. Pour into ramekins. Place cups in a large glass baking dish. Sprinkle with nutmeg. Pour warm water into baking dish until halfway up sides of ramekins. Bake at 275 degrees 20-30 minutes or until tester comes out clean. Do not overcook. Cool. Cover each ramekin with plastic wrap and refrigerate.

SERVES 6

Excellent by itself or served with berries.

Patricia Harris, grandmother of several HIES students, shared this recipe with me several years ago. Whole milk works best.

COCONUT FLAN

1 cup sugar
½ cup water
2 cups milk
2 cups heavy cream

1 cup shredded coconut
1 cinnamon stick
1 cup sweetened coconut milk

10 egg yolks
Toasted coconut, lemon zest and
    blueberries for garnish

Combine sugar and water in a heavy saucepan over low heat. Cook and stir until sugar caramelizes and is rich golden browned. Pour caramel into 6-8 heat proof flan or pudding cups. Cool.

Combine milk, heavy cream, coconut and cinnamon stick in a saucepan. Simmer gently 30 minutes. Remove cinnamon stick. Cool 15 minutes. Stir in coconut milk. Beat egg yolks in a bowl. Whisk in ½ cup hot milk. Whisk egg mixture into remaining milk mixture. Pour coconut mixture into a large heat proof measuring cup. Place flan cups in a large baking dish. Place dish on middle rack of oven. Divide coconut mixture among flan cups. Pour warm water around cups into baking dish. Avoid splashing into flan cups. Bake at 350 degrees 45-50 minutes. Cool completely. Refrigerate 6-8 hours or overnight.

To serve, run a sharp knife around the outside of the flan to loosen. Invert cup on a plate and pop out flan. Garnish with toasted coconut, lemon zest and fresh blueberries.

SERVES 6-8

EASY FRUIT COBBLER

2 cups fruit of choice
1 stick unsalted butter, sliced into pats

¾ cup all-purpose flour
2 teaspoons baking powder
Dash of salt

1 cup sugar
¾ cup milk

Place fruit in bottom of 11 x 7 x 2-inch baking dish. Scatter butter over fruit. Combine flour, baking powder, salt and sugar. Stir in milk until smooth. Pour batter evenly over fruit. Bake at 350 degrees about 30 minutes until golden browned. Cool slightly. Serve warm with a scoop of vanilla ice cream.

SERVES 6-8

Sliced peaches and blueberries are perfect.

To cobble means to throw together hastily and clumsily.

MACADAMIA NUT AND COCONUT TART

2 cups macadamia nuts
Pastry for single crust
1 cup shredded coconut flakes
4 eggs

½ cup sugar
½ cup packed light brown sugar
1 cup light corn syrup
½ teaspoon vanilla

⅛ teaspoon salt
4 tablespoons butter, melted
1 tablespoon all-purpose flour
8 scoops vanilla ice cream

Toast nuts on a baking sheet at 375 degrees 8-10 minutes until golden browned. Cool completely. Coarsely chop nuts. Line a 10 inch tart pan with pastry dough. Sprinkle nuts and coconut over pastry. Beat eggs in a bowl. Add sugar, brown sugar, corn syrup, vanilla, salt, butter and flour. Mix well. Pour mixture over nuts and coconut. Place tart pan on a baking sheet. Bake at 375 degrees 45-50 minutes or until filling sets. Cool completely. Serve each piece with a scoop of ice cream.

SERVES 8

ENGLISH TRIFLE
(GOOD AT CHRISTMAS TIME)

Pound cake, cut into ½ inch slices

⅓ cup golden sherry

1 package (12 ounce) frozen raspberries, thawed, reserving juice

2 packages (3 ounces each) cook and serve vanilla pudding mix, prepared

Heavy cream, whipped or Cool Whip

½ cup toasted slivered almonds

Drizzle sherry and raspberry juice over cake slices. Arrange three-fourths cake over bottom and up sides of a trifle dish. Place half raspberries on top. Spoon half pudding over raspberries. Arrange second cake layer. Top with remaining raspberries and pudding. Cover with whipped cream or Cool Whip. Cover and refrigerate for several hours. Sprinkle with almonds before serving.

SERVES 10

May substitute frozen strawberries, thawed and bananas for raspberries.

 # GOLDEN BEAR ONE MINUTE SNACK MIX

Assorted Teddy Grahams (cinnamon, honey or chocolate)

Cheerios

Honeycomb cereal

Raisins

Mini pretzels

Semi-sweet chocolate chips

Gummy bears (optional)

Combine Teddy Grahams, Cheerios, Honeycomb cereal, raisins, pretzels, chocolate chips and gummy bears. Mix well.

SERVES 6-8

Kahlúa Flan

¾ cup sugar
4 large eggs
1 can (14 ounce) sweetened
condensed milk

1 can (12 ounce) evaporated milk
2 tablespoons Kahlúa or other
coffee flavored liqueur

Mexican chocolate shavings and
cocoa powder for garnish

Cook sugar over medium heat until sugar begins to melt in a small saucepan. Reduce heat and swirl the saucepan until sugar caramelizes and is golden browned. Do not stir or touch the sugar. Swirl the pan to melt evenly. Pour sugar into a metal flan mold or 9 inch round cake pan. Turn pan until bottom is evenly coated. Cool and allow sugar to harden.

Place mold or cake pan in a large roasting pan. Pour hot water into roasting pan to reach halfway to sides of pan. Whisk eggs in a bowl. Pour in condensed milk, evaporated milk and Kahlúa. Mix well. Pour milk mixture into mold. Bake at 350 degrees 50-60 minutes or until firm in center but still jiggles slightly. Cool on wire rack. Refrigerate at least 2 hours.

To serve, run a thin sharp knife around rim of flan. Place a platter or large plate on top of flan. Gently invert pan. Lift away pan. Top with chocolate shaving and cocoa. Cut into wedges and serve immediately.

Serves 8-10

KEY LIME CHEESECAKE BARS

CRUST
1½ cups all-purpose flour

⅔ cup powdered sugar

¼ teaspoon salt

1½ sticks cold butter, cut into 12 pieces

FILLING
2 packages (8 ounces each) cream cheese, softened

⅔ cup sugar

3 eggs

⅓ cup lime juice

½ teaspoon vanilla

Powdered sugar for garnish

CRUST

Combine flour, powdered sugar and salt. Cut in butter with pastry blender or two knives until crumbly. Press mixture into a lightly greased 13 x 9 x 2-inch baking dish. Bake at 350 degrees 15 minutes. Cool 10 minutes.

FILLING

Beat cream cheese and sugar until smooth. Add eggs, one at a time, beating well after each addition. Beat in lime juice and vanilla. Pour filling over crust. Bake 22-28 minutes or until firm. Cool to room temperature. Cover and refrigerate overnight. Cut into squares. Sprinkle with powered sugar.

SERVES 12-15

May garnish with crushed almonds or lime glaze or chocolate glaze.

LEMON CHIFFON PIE

CRUST

1½ cups graham cracker crumbs

⅓ cup powdered sugar

1 stick butter, melted

FILLING

1 package gelatin

¼ cup cold water

½ cup sugar

½ cup lemon juice

½ teaspoon salt

4 egg yolks, beaten

1 teaspoon lemon zest

4 egg whites

½ cup sugar

Heavy cream, whipped

CRUST

Combine cracker crumbs, powdered sugar and butter until crumbly. Press mixture into bottom and up sides of a 9 inch pie plate. Refrigerate until firm.

FILLING

Dissolve gelatin in water. Set aside. Combine sugar, lemon juice, salt and egg yolks in top of double boiler. Cook over boiling water until thickened. Add gelatin and lemon zest. Cool mixture. Beat egg whites until stiff and dry. Gently fold in sugar. Fold egg white mixture into custard. Pour filling into crust. Refrigerate until set. Serve with whipped cream.

SERVES 8

 MIXED BERRY CRUMBLE

2 packages (10 ounces each) frozen berries, thawed, any mixture of blueberries, raspberries or strawberries

1 package (18 ounce) yellow cake mix

1 stick butter, softened

Pour berries into a greased 13 x 9 x 2-inch baking dish. Combine cake mix and butter until crumbly. Sprinkle mixture evenly over berries. Bake at 350 degrees 30-40 minutes or until golden browned.

SERVES 12

Great recipe for kids to make!

PUMPKIN CHIFFON PIE

⅓ cup milk

6 tablespoons brown sugar

⅓ teaspoons salt

1½ teaspoons cinnamon

⅓ teaspoon ground ginger

½ teaspoon ground allspice

1 cup canned pumpkin

2½ ounces envelopes unflavored gelatin (2 packets)

3 tablespoons cold water

3 egg whites, beaten

6 teaspoons sugar

1 (9 inch) graham cracker pie crust

Combine milk, brown sugar, salt, cinnamon, ginger, allspice and pumpkin in a saucepan. Cook over low heat, stirring until boiling. Boil 1 minute. Remove from heat. Cool in refrigerator.

Dissolve gelatin in cold water. Stir into pumpkin mixture. Beat egg whites until fluffy, while slowly adding sugar. Gradually stir into pumpkin mixture. Pour filling into crust. Refrigerate 3 hours.

SERVES 8

Friends and family who do not usually like Pumpkin Pie love this recipe. It is light and delicious!

MY FAVORITE PECAN PIE

1 cup dark corn syrup

3 eggs

1 cup sugar

3 tablespoons butter, melted

1 teaspoon vanilla

1-2 tablespoons Kahlúa

1½ cups pecans, chopped

1 (9 inch) pie crust, unbaked

Combine corn syrup, eggs, sugar, butter, vanilla and Kahlúa. Mix well. Stir in pecans. Pour filling into crust. Bake on center rack at 350 degrees 55-60 minutes. Cool 2 hours. Serve warm with ice cream.

SERVES 8

This pie gets rave reviews every time.

POTS DE CRÈME

1 cup semi-sweet chocolate chips
1 egg

2 tablespoons sugar
1 teaspoon vanilla

Dash of salt
¾ cup milk

Combine chocolate chips, egg, sugar, vanilla and salt in a blender. Blend until well combined. Heat milk just to boiling. Slowly add to blender on low speed. Blend 1 minute. Pour mixture into serving cups. Refrigerate at least 1 hour.

SERVES 2-4

May also freeze. Remove from freezer and place in refrigerator several hours before serving.

TIRAMISU

6 large egg yolks
6-8 tablespoons sugar
35 ounces mascarpone cheese

6 egg whites, stiffly beaten
Ladyfingers
1 cup strong espresso

3-4 ounces very finely chopped
   bittersweet chocolate
⅔ cup Marsarsla

Beat egg yolks until very light. Gradually beat in sugar. Beat in mascarpone cheese until thickened like whipped cream. Gently fold in egg whites. Dip enough ladyfingers in cooled espresso until softened and line bottom of 13 x 9 x 2-inch baking dish. Cover with half chocolate. Spread with half mascarpone mixture. Dip second layer ladyfingers in Marsala until slightly softened. Arrange over mascarpone layer. Cover with remaining mascarpone mixture. Top with remaining chocolate. Refrigerate several hours.

SERVES 12-15

NANAIMO BARS

CRUST

1 stick butter	1 egg, slightly beaten	1 cup fine coconut
¼ cup sugar	1 teaspoon vanilla	½ cup crushed nuts
5 tablespoons cocoa powder	2 cups crushed graham crackers	

FILLING

2 cups powdered sugar	2 tablespoons custard powder	Milk
1 stick butter, melted		

TOPPING

4 squares semi-sweet chocolate	1 tablespoon butter

CRUST

Melt butter, sugar and cocoa in top of double boiler. Stir in egg, vanilla, cracker crumbs, coconut and nuts. Mix well. Press mixture into a well greased 13 x 9 x 2-inch baking dish.

FILLING

Blend powdered sugar, butter, custard powder and enough milk to spreading consistency. Spread over crust. Refrigerate 15 minutes.

TOPPING

Melt chocolate squares and butter until smooth. Pour topping over filling. Refrigerate until set.

SERVES 12-15

ROSE'S LEMON MERINGUE PIE

FILLING

1½ cups sugar

⅓ cup plus 1 tablespoon cornstarch

1½ cups water

3 egg yolks, slightly beaten

3 tablespoons butter

2 teaspoons lemon zest

½ cup lemon juice

1 (9 inch) pie crust, baked

MERINGUE

¼ teaspoon cream of tartar

6 tablespoons sugar

3 egg whites, room temperature

½ teaspoon vanilla

FILLING

Blend sugar and cornstarch in a saucepan. Stir in water. Cook over low to medium heat, stirring constantly, until mixture boils and thickens. Boil 1 minute. Remove from heat. Gradually stir half warm mixture into egg yolks in a bowl. Stir egg mixture into warm mixture. Return to heat. Bring to boil. Boil 1 minute. Remove from heat. Stir in butter, lemon zest and lemon juice. Pour filling into pie crust.

MERINGUE

Combine cream of tartar and sugar in a small bowl. Beat egg whites in a separate bowl until frothy. Very gradually add sugar and vanilla, beating until stiff peaks form. Gently spoon meringue over filling, covering entire pie to all edges without any air pockets.

Bake at 375 degrees 10 minutes or until meringue just begins to brown. Cool pie gradually by turning off heat and opening oven door. Cool 15 minutes in oven. Cool to room temperature before storing in refrigerator.

SERVES 8

CAKES
AND COOKIES

CARROT CAKE

CAKE

2 cups all-purpose flour
2 teaspoons baking soda
2 teaspoons cinnamon
½ teaspoon salt
3 eggs, beaten

¾ cup vegetable oil
¾ cup buttermilk
2 cups sugar
2 teaspoons vanilla

1 can (8 ounce) crushed pineapple, drained
2 cups grated carrots
1 can (3½ ounce) flaked coconut
1 cup coarsely chopped nuts

BUTTERMILK GLAZE

1 cup sugar
½ teaspoon baking soda

½ cup buttermilk
1 stick butter

1 tablespoon light corn syrup
1 teaspoon vanilla

CREAM CHEESE FROSTING

1 stick butter, softened
1 package (8 ounce) cream cheese, softened

1 teaspoon vanilla
2 cups powdered sugar

1 teaspoon orange juice
1 teaspoon orange zest

CAKE

Sift together flour, baking soda, cinnamon and salt. Combine eggs, oil, buttermilk, sugar and vanilla in a mixer bowl. Beat until well blended. Mix in flour mixture. Add pineapple, carrots, coconut and nuts. Mix well. Pour batter into two (9 inch) cake pans. Bake at 350 degrees 55 minutes or until tester comes out clean.

BUTTERMILK GLAZE

Combine sugar, baking soda, buttermilk, butter and corn syrup in a saucepan. Bring to boil. Reduce heat and simmer 5 minutes, stirring occasionally. Watch carefully to not boil over. Remove from heat. Stir in vanilla. Pour warm glaze over hot cake layers. Cool in pans about 15 minutes until glaze is totally absorbed. Remove from pans and cool completely.

CREAM CHEESE FROSTING

Cream butter and cream cheese until fluffy. Add vanilla, powdered sugar, orange juice and orange zest. Mix until smooth. Frost cooled cake. Refrigerate until frosting is set. Serve cake cold.

SERVES 15

May be made a day in advance and stored covered in refrigerator.

CARAMEL CHEESECAKE BRÛLÉE

2 packages (8 ounces each) cream
  cheese, softened

2 tablespoons sour cream

2 eggs

¼ cup heavy cream

½ cup sugar

¾ cup graham cracker crumbs

⅓ cup ground toasted pecans

2 tablespoons unsalted butter,
  melted and cooled

3 tablespoons sugar

½ cup Michael Ricchiuti caramel
  sauce

8 teaspoons sugar

Beat cream cheese and sour cream until smooth. Add eggs, cream and sugar. Beat until well blended. In a separate bowl, combine cracker crumbs, pecans, butter and sugar until crumbly. Divide mixture among 4 lightly buttered mini springform pans. Press into bottom of each pan. Drizzle 2 tablespoons caramel sauce over each crust. Divide filling among four pans and spread evenly. Bake at 325 degrees 15-20 minutes until set. Cool on wire racks to room temperature. Refrigerate at least 3 hours. To serve, unmold cheesecakes and sprinkle each with 2 teaspoons sugar over surface. With a kitchen torch, move flame continuously in small circles over surface until sugar melts and browned.

SERVES 4 MINI CHEESECAKES

CHOCOLATE CHIP BUNDT CAKE

1 package (18 ounce) yellow cake
  mix

1 package (4 ounce) instant
  chocolate pudding mix

4 large eggs

1 container (8 ounce) sour cream

½ cup sugar

¾ cup vegetable oil

¾ cup water

1 cup milk chocolate chips

Beat cake mix, pudding mix, eggs, sour cream, sugar, oil and water with electric mixer until smooth. Stir in chocolate chips. Pour batter into a greased and floured Bundt pan. Bake at 350 degrees 1 hour.

SERVES 12-15

I have given this recipe to so many people all over Atlanta, that my friend who gave it me refuses to give me any more recipes! Thank you Alicia, we love the cake!

Cheesecake

CRUST

2 cups graham cracker crumbs

½ teaspoon cinnamon

½ teaspoon salt

¼ cup chopped pecans or walnuts

½ cup sugar

1 stick butter, melted

FILLING

3 eggs

1 cup sugar

2 packages (8 ounces each) cream cheese, softened

2 teaspoons vanilla

1 teaspoon almond extract

¼ teaspoon salt

3 cups sour cream

CRUST

Combine crumbs, cinnamon, salt, pecans and sugar in a 9 inch springform pan. Pour in butter and mix well. Remove 3 tablespoons mixture for topping. Press remaining mixture over bottom and 2½ inches up sides.

FILLING

Beat eggs and sugar with mixer or food processor. Add cream cheese, vanilla, almond extract and salt. Mix until smooth. Fold in sour cream. Pour filling over crust. Sprinkle with reserved crumbs. Bake at 375 degrees about 45 minutes or until cheesecake begins to crack around edges and center is set. Cool. Refrigerate before serving.

SERVES 12-16

Cream Cheese Pound Cake

3 sticks butter, softened

1 package (8 ounce) cream cheese, softened

3 cups sugar

6 large eggs

1½ teaspoons vanilla

3 cups all-purpose flour

⅛ teaspoon salt

Beat butter and cream cheese until creamy. Gradually beat in sugar. Beat 5-7 minutes. Add eggs, one at a time, beating just until yellow disappears. Add vanilla and mix well. Combine flour and salt. Gradually beat into creamed mixture just until blended. Pour batter into a greased and floured 10 inch tube pan. Place 2 cups water into a glass ovenproof measuring cup in oven. Bake cake at 300 degrees 1 hour, 30 minutes.

SERVES 12-15

Gâteau Au Chocolat

CAKE

2 sticks butter

1 cup milk chocolate chips

3 ounces unsweetened chocolate, chopped

4 eggs

1¼ cups sugar

1 tablespoon all-purpose flour

1 tablespoon vanilla

1 cup coarsely chopped walnuts

CHOCOLATE GLAZE

4 tablespoons butter

2 ounces semi-sweet chocolate, chopped or ⅓ cup chocolate chips

2 ounces unsweetened chocolate, chopped

2 teaspoons light corn syrup

12-16 walnut halves

CAKE

Butter bottom and 1 inch up sides of a 9 inch springform pan. Wrap a 12 inch square piece of foil around bottom and up the outside of pan.

Combine butter, chocolate chips and unsweetened chocolate pieces in a saucepan. Cook over low heat, stirring constantly, until chocolate melts. Whisk eggs in a bowl. Whisk in sugar and flour. Add vanilla. Slowly mix in chocolate mixture. Stir in walnuts. Pour mixture into pan. Place pan in a large baking dish. Pour boiling water into dish to depth of ½ inch. Bake at 325 degrees about 1 hour or until tester comes out with a few moist crumbs. Remove springform pan from water. Cool completely on wire rack.

CHOCOLATE GLAZE

Combine butter, semi-sweet chocolate, unsweetened chocolate and corn syrup in a heavy saucepan. Cook and stir over low heat until chocolate melts. Remove from heat and cool to room temperature, stirring occasionally. Beat with wire whisk until slightly thickened. Carefully loosen springform pans sides and remove cake. Pour glaze over cake and smooth carefully with a metal spatula. Quickly decorate cake with walnut halves. Let glaze set. Cover and refrigerate until ready to serve. Remove from refrigerator about 15 minutes before serving.

SERVES 12-16

GLAZED LEMON CAKE

CAKE

2 sticks sweet butter, softened
2 cups sugar
3 eggs

3 cups unbleached all-purpose flour, sifted
½ teaspoon baking soda
½ teaspoon salt

1 cup buttermilk
2 tightly packed tablespoons lemon zest
2 tablespoons lemon juice

LEMON ICING

1 package (16 ounce) powdered sugar

1 stick sweet butter, softened
3 tightly packed tablespoons lemon zest

½ cup lemon juice

CAKE

Cream butter and sugar until light and fluffy. Add eggs, one at a time, beating well after each addition. Sift together flour, baking soda and salt. Stir flour mixture alternately with buttermilk into creamed mixture, beginning and ending with flour mixture. Stir in lemon zest and lemon juice.

Pour batter into a greased 10 inch tube pan. Set on middle rack. Bake at 325 degrees 1 hour, 5 minutes or until cake pulls away from side of pan and tester comes out clean. Cool in pan 10 minutes. Remove cake from pan.

LEMON ICING

Cream powdered sugar and butter until smooth. Stir in lemon zest and lemon juice. Spread icing over warm cake.

SERVES 8-10

Use a microplane zester for lemon zest.

LEMON CAKE SUPREME

CAKE

1 package (18 ounce) lemon supreme cake mix

½ cup sugar
½ cup vegetable oil

1 cup apricot nectar
4 eggs

GLAZE

1 package (8 ounce) powdered sugar

2 tablespoons lemon juice
1 lemon, zested

1 tablespoon butter, melted

CAKE

Combine cake mix, sugar, oil, nectar and eggs until smooth. Pour batter into a greased and floured tube pan. Bake at 350 degrees 45 minutes. Cool 10 minutes in pan. Invert and place on serving platter.

GLAZE

Blend powdered sugar, lemon juice, lemon zest and butter. Pour glaze over warm cake.

SERVES 12-15

GRANDMA BROWN'S POUND CAKE

2 sticks butter or margarine
2 cups sugar

6 eggs
1 teaspoon almond extract or vanilla

2 cups all-purpose flour

Cream butter and sugar until smooth. Add eggs, one at a time, beating well after each addition. Stir in almond extract. Gradually beat in flour until creamy. Pour batter into a greased tube pan. Bake at 300 degrees 1 hour, 20 minutes.

SERVES 12-15

PRALINE AND GOAT CHEESE CHEESECAKE WITH PRALINE SAUCE AND CANDIED PECANS

PRALINES

1 package (8 ounce) light brown sugar
Dash of salt

¼ cup plus 2 tablespoons evaporated milk

1½ teaspoons butter
1 cup chopped pecans

CHEESECAKE

2 cups graham cracker crumbs
½ cup chopped roasted pecans
1½ sticks butter, melted
3 packages (8 ounces each) cream cheese, softened

8 ounces goat cheese, softened
1½ cups sugar
1 cup sour cream
3 eggs

1 tablespoon cornstarch
¼ cup heavy cream
1 cup crushed pralines
1 teaspoon vanilla

TOPPING

¼ cup sour cream
¼ cup goat cheese, softened
3 tablespoons honey

¼ cup graham cracker crumbs
1 cup praline sauce or caramel sauce

1 cup candied pecans
Whipped cream
Mint sprigs for garnish

PRALINES

Combine brown sugar, salt, milk and butter in a heavy saucepan. Cook over low heat, stirring constantly with a wooden spoon, until sugar dissolves. Stir in pecans. Cook over medium heat until mixture reaches soft ball stage of 234-240 degrees on candy thermometer. Place a drop of boiling syrup in ice water and it will form a soft ball. Remove from heat. Stir rapidly until mixture thickens. Drop syrup by teaspoonfuls 1 inch apart onto parchment paper-lined baking sheets. Cool completely until set. Store in an airtight container.

CHEESECAKE

Combine cracker crumbs, pecans and butter. Press mixture into the bottom and up sides of a 10 inch springform pan.

Blend cream cheese, goat cheese, sugar and sour cream in a food processor until smooth. Add eggs, one at a time, blending well after each addition. Whisk cornstarch into cream. Stir into filling. Crush pralines to equal 1 cup. Fold in pralines and vanilla. Pour filling over crust. Bake at 350 degrees 1 hour or until set. Remove from oven. Run a knife around rim of cake to prevent cracking.

Praline and Goat Cheese Cheesecake with Praline Sauce and Candied Pecans, continued

TOPPING
Blend sour cream, goat cheese and honey until smooth. Spread evenly over top of cake. Sprinkle with cracker crumbs. To serve, place a cake slice on a plate. Drizzle with praline sauce. Sprinkle pecans around plate. Place whipped cream in a pastry bag with a star tip and pipe whipped cream over cake. Garnish with mint sprigs.

SERVES 12-15

KAHLÚA CAKE

1 package (18 ounce) yellow cake mix

1 package (3 ounce) instant chocolate pudding mix

4 eggs

1 cup vegetable oil

⅓ cup Kahlúa

⅓ cup vodka

½ cup sugar

¾ cup water

¼ cup Kahlúa

½ cup powdered sugar

Combine cake mix, pudding mix, eggs and oil. Beat until smooth. Add Kahlúa, vodka, sugar and water. Mix well. Batter will be thin. Spoon batter into a greased and floured Bundt pan. Bake at 350 degrees 50 minutes or until tester comes out clean. Cool in pan several minutes. Invert cake pan and place cake on a serving platter. Blend Kahlúa and powdered sugar until smooth. Drizzle glaze over warm cake. Cool completely.

SERVES 12-15

This cake freezes well.

PUMPKIN CAKE

1 can (16 ounce) pumpkin
1 cup vegetable oil
2 cups sugar

2 cups all-purpose flour
4 eggs
2 teaspoons cinnamon

2 teaspoons baking soda
1 teaspoon salt

Combine pumpkin, oil, sugar, flour, eggs, cinnamon, baking soda and salt. Mix well. Pour batter into a lightly greased Bundt pan. Bake at 350 degrees 55 minutes or until tester comes out clean. Cool completely. Invert onto a serving platter.

SERVES 16-25

Easy and may be prepared in advance. May also be frozen.

OREO AND FUDGE ICE CREAM CAKE

½ cup fudge ice cream topping, warm
1 container (8 ounce) frozen whipped topping, thawed

1 package (4 ounce) instant chocolate pudding mix

8 Oreo sandwich cookies, chopped
12 vanilla ice cream sandwiches

Blend fudge topping and 1 cup whipped topping until smooth. Stir in pudding mix. Add ¼ cup milk if too thick.

Add cookie crumbs. Arrange four ice cream sandwiches side by side on a 24 x 12-inch piece of foil. Spread half pudding mixture over sandwiches. Repeat layers. Top next layer with pudding mixture. Spread remaining top and sides with whipped topping. Bring up sides of foil and loosely seal. Freeze at least 4 hours. Soften slightly before serving.

SERVES 12

Great for kids to make.

RED VELVET CAKE

2 eggs

1½ cups sugar

1½ cups vegetable oil or melted butter

1 teaspoon vinegar

2½ cups all-purpose flour or cake flour

1 teaspoon baking soda

1 cup buttermilk

1 teaspoon vanilla

2 tablespoons red food coloring

Beat eggs. Add sugar, oil and vinegar. Mix well. Sift together flour and baking soda. Add to creamed mixture. Stir in buttermilk, vanilla and food coloring. Divide batter between two cake pans. Bake at 350 degrees 25 minutes. Frost with cream cheese frosting.

SERVES 12

May double the recipe and make four layers for a nicer looking cake.

KEY LIME PIE

1 package (8 ounce) cream cheese, softened

1 can (14 ounce) sweetened condensed milk

1 teaspoon vanilla

⅓ cup Key lime juice

1 (9 inch) graham cracker crust

Whipped cream for garnish

Blend cream cheese, milk, vanilla and lime juice until smooth. Pour filling into crust. Refrigerate. Top with whipped cream prior to serving.

SERVES 8

A friend actually sells this to restaurants. It is delicious and extremely easy.

MOCHA CAKE WITH BUTTER CREAM FROSTING

CAKE

2 cups sugar

2 cups all-purpose flour

¾ cup cocoa powder

2 teaspoons baking soda

1½ teaspoons salt

2 eggs

⅔ cup vegetable oil

2 teaspoons vanilla

2 cups hot strong coffee

BUTTER CREAM FROSTING

1 package (16 ounce) powdered sugar

1 teaspoon vanilla or almond extract

1 stick butter, softened

1 tablespoon milk

CAKE

Combine sugar, flour, cocoa, baking soda and salt. Make a well in center of dry ingredients. Add eggs, oil, vanilla and coffee to well. Mix until smooth. Pour batter into a 13 x 9 x 2-inch baking dish or two 9 inch pans. Bake at 350 degrees 40 minutes.

BUTTER CREAM FROSTING

Blend powdered sugar, vanilla, butter and milk until creamy. Frost cake.

SERVES 12

HOLY INNOCENTS' EPISCOPAL SCHOOL LUNCH ROOM BUTTER COOKIES

4 sticks butter, softened

2 cups powdered sugar

4½ cups all-purpose flour, sifted

2 teaspoons vanilla

1 cup chopped pecans

Powdered sugar

Cream butter and powdered sugar until smooth. Gradually mix in flour. Stir in vanilla and pecans. Mix well. Roll dough into 3 inch balls. Place on baking sheet about 1½ inches apart. Press down with fork. Bake at 350 degrees 20 minutes. Remove from oven and sprinkle with powdered sugar.

SERVES 3-4 DOZEN

CHASE'S MAGIC NO BAKE COOKIES

3 cups graham cracker crumbs   1 cup sweetened condensed milk   ¾ cup milk chocolate chips

Combine cracker crumbs and milk until moistened. Stir in chocolate chips. Roll tablespoonfuls of dough into balls. Place on wax-lined baking sheets. Refrigerate until set.

SERVES 8

Easy, delicious and very child friendly!

FORGOTTEN COOKIES

2 egg whites, room temperature   Dash of salt   1 cup semi-sweet chocolate chips
⅔ cup sugar   1 teaspoon vanilla

Beat egg whites until stiff. Add sugar, one tablespoon at a time. Add salt and vanilla. Fold in chocolate chips. Drop dough onto a foil-lined baking sheet. Place in a 350 degree oven and immediately turn oven off. Leave in oven 8 hours.

SERVES 8

PEANUT BUTTER CHOCOLATE CHIP COOKIES

1 cup creamy peanut butter   1 egg   ½ cup mini chocolate chips
1 cup sugar   1 teaspoon vanilla

Combine peanut butter, sugar, egg, vanilla and chocolate chips. Roll dough into tablespoon size balls. Place on greased baking sheet. Flatten with a large fork. Bake at 350 degrees 12 minutes.

SERVES 2 DOZEN

HOLIDAY SUGAR COOKIES

1½ cups all-purpose flour
1 teaspoon baking powder
¼ teaspoon salt

1 stick unsalted butter, softened
¾ cup sugar
1 egg

1½ teaspoons vanilla
Colored sugar for decorating

Combine flour, baking powder and salt. Mix well. In a separate bowl, beat butter and sugar with an electric mixer until light and fluffy. Add egg and vanilla. Beat until well blended. Gradually blend in flour mixture. Cover and refrigerate at least 1 hour until firm. Roll dough out on a lightly floured surface into a large circle about ⅛ inch thick. Cut dough with cookie cutters of choice. Transfer to lightly greased baking sheets. Roll and cut dough until used up. Sprinkle with colored sugar. Bake at 350 degrees 10-12 minutes until lightly golden browned. Transfer to rack and cool completely.

SERVES 3 DOZEN

MAPLE PECAN COOKIES

2 sticks unsalted butter, softened
½ cup sugar
1 large egg yolk

2 tablespoons maple syrup
½ teaspoon vanilla

2 cups all-purpose flour
1¼ cups coarsely chopped pecans

Beat butter 3 minutes until pale and creamy. Gradually beat in sugar until well blended. In a separate bowl, whisk egg yolk, maple syrup and vanilla. Drizzle mixture into butter, beating on low speed until blended.

Using a wooden spoon, stir in flour and pecans. Divide dough in half and shape into two disks. Wrap each disk with plastic wrap. Refrigerate at least 2 hours or overnight. Let dough stand at room temperature 10 minutes.

Roll out each disk between two sheets of wax paper to ¼ inch thickness. Cut with 2 inch cookie cutter. Place on parchment paper-lined baking sheets. Bake at 325 degrees 20-25 minutes or until golden browned. Cool on wire racks.

SERVES 3½ DOZEN

MOLASSES SUGAR COOKIES

¾ cup shortening

1 cup sugar

¼ cup molasses

1 egg

2 teaspoons baking soda

2 cups sifted all-purpose flour

½ teaspoon ground cloves

½ teaspoon ground ginger

1 teaspoon cinnamon

½ teaspoon salt

Colored sugar

Melt shortening in 3-4 quart saucepan over low heat. Remove from heat. Cool. Beat in sugar, molasses and egg. Sift together flour, baking soda, cloves, ginger, cinnamon and salt. Stir into creamed mixture. Mix well. Refrigerate at least 2 hours. Shape dough into 1 inch balls. Roll in colored sugar and place 2 inches apart on greased baking sheets. Bake at 375 degrees 8-10 minutes.

SERVES 5 DOZEN

Kids love to roll the balls in colored sugar.

PECAN SANDIES

2 sticks butter, softened

⅓ cup sugar

2 teaspoons water

2 teaspoons vanilla

2 cups sifted all-purpose flour

1 cup chopped pecans

Powdered sugar

Cream butter and sugar. Add water and vanilla. Slowly stir in flour until blended. Add pecans and mix well. Shape dough into a 2 inch log. Wrap in wax paper. Refrigerate 3-4 hours. Cut dough into 1 inch slices. Shape into balls and place 1 inch apart on ungreased baking sheet.

Bake at 325 degrees 20 minutes. Cool enough to touch. Place warm cookie in powdered sugar and toss to coat. Store in airtight container with wax paper between layers.

SERVES 3-4 DOZEN

WEDDING COOKIES

2 sticks butter, softened
½ cup powdered sugar
½ teaspoon vanilla

¼ teaspoon salt
1¾ cups all-purpose flour

½ cup chopped pecans
Powdered sugar

Cream butter. Stir in powdered sugar, vanilla and salt. Slowly mix in flour and pecans. Shape dough into small balls. Place on an ungreased baking sheet. Bake at 350 degrees 15 minutes or until lightly browned. Cool on wire rack. Place powdered sugar in a bag. Add several cookies and shake until well coated.

SERVES 3 DOZEN

May store in refrigerator until ready to bake.

WHIPPED SHORTBREAD

4 sticks butter, softened
1 cup powdered sugar

½ cup cornstarch
1 teaspoon vanilla

3 cups all-purpose flour

Beat together butter, powdered sugar, cornstarch and vanilla until consistency of whipped cream. Beat in flour. Drop dough by spoonfuls onto greased and floured baking sheet. Bake at 350 degrees 12-15 minutes.

SERVES 3-4 DOZEN

MENUS

EASTER DINNER

Tarragon-Chive Deviled Eggs

Graham's Brie En Croûte

Grilled Butterflied Leg of Lamb

Asian Asparagus

Cindy's Wild Rice

Carrot Cake

AFTER THE GAME

Healthy and Delicious Trail Mix

Bear Mix

Crispy Chicken Fingers

Summer Pizza

Vegetable Platter with Ranch Dressing

Fruit Salad

Peanut Butter
Chocolate Chip Cookies

Oreo and Fudge
Ice Cream Cake

WILD GAME DINNER MENU

Baby Arugula Salad

Grilled Creole Quail

Pecan Crusted Venison

Southern Cooked Greens

Cane Syrup Bread Pudding

BEACH MENU

Dark and Stormy Cocktails

Conch Fritters with
Mango Chutney

Frogmore Stew

Macadamia Nut and
Coconut Tart

SOUL FOOD MENU

Pan-Fried Chicken with Bacon

Southern Cooked Greens

Black-Eyed Peas

Cat-Head Biscuits

Banana Pudding

CINCO DE MAYO MENU

Tomato Avocado Salad with
Lime and Toasted Cumin

Yucatan Marinated Grouper

Classic Mexican Fried Beans

Kahlúa Flan

CUBAN MENU

Mojito

Instant Black Bean Soup

Taylor's Pressed Cubano Sandwiches
(appetizer portion)

Paella

Coconut Flan

ITALIAN DINNER MENU

Bruschetta with Frisée, Prosciutto and Mozzarella

Mixed Greens and Goat Cheese

Rotini with Salmon and Roasted Garlic

Tiramisu

Serve with Italian bread

We recommend an elegant and delicate Italian wine such as a Pinto Bianco or Pinot Grigio to enhance the richness of the fish and the sweetness of the roasted garlic.

SOUTHWESTERN PARTY

Black Bean Salsa

Tomato, Avocado Salad with Lime and Toasted Cumin

Southwestern Grilled Chicken Fajitas

Roasted Asparagus

Key Lime Cheesecake Bars and
Chocolate Toffee Bars

Mojitos, Mexican Beer and Wine

For festive decorations, use many colored peppers to fill and line clear pillar candleholders around candles.
Place Mexican beer in a tub filled with ice. Tie a piece of raffia into a bow around the neck of the beer and attach a toothpick with lime to the raffia.

THANKSGIVING MENU

Lila's Goat Cheese Torte

Roast Turkey

Aunt Ruth's Hen and Cornbread Dressing

Cranberry Sauce

Squash Casserole

Green Beans with Tomato and Fresh Basil

Ginger Carrots

Pumpkin Chiffon Pie

CHRISTMAS MENU

Blood Orange Juice with Champagne (Christmas Mimosa)

"Bruschetta" Salmon Spread

Raspberry Brie

Mixed Greens and Strawberry Salad

Beef Tenderloin

Potato Casserole

Spinach Madeline

English Trifle

MEXICAN MENU

Chips & Salsa

Seven Layer Mexican Dip

Mexican Chicken Tinga

Mexican Rice

Kahlúa Flan

ACKNOWLEDGEMENTS

RECIPE CONTRIBUTORS

Alice Adams

Louisa Affleck

Gary Baldwin

Lottie Bolton

Nora Borne

Janella Brand

Caroline Brumbeloe

Fran Buckland

Leslie Burns

Karen Calhoun

Alyson Cohen

Wendy Cook

Shannon Cullens

Mary Frances Davidson

Winston Dees

Lizzie Duncan

Kimberly Earle

Brenda Farmer

Lori Fisher-Maitski

Grace France

J. Russell Frank

Kerri Glatting

Robin Gleason

Tijana Graham

Delaine Griffin

Katharine Hamer

McLean Hamer

Jayne Hammond

Leah Henry

Beth Hereford

Lizzie Humphrey Lee

Kathleen Keeler

Shannon Kelsey

Carmen Kissack

Courtney Lewis

Gerri Lewis

Bonnie Lu

Carol Luther

Greg Lyles

Ann Magruder

Alice Malcolm

Ellen Massie

Julie Maxman

Deborah McCarty

Allison McClymont

Judy McGrew

Becky McMinn

Suzanne Mellot

Maribel Menay

Tracy Merrill

Barb Meyer

Amy Mitchell

Elaine Moore

Michelle Nelson

Rita Peery

Robin Phillips

Jude Rasmus

Karen Rolader

Beth Rousseau

Linda Saca

Susan Sapronov

Stacy Scott

Lila Shirley

Misty Smith

Linda Sprinkle

Dorothy Sullivan

Rosemary Tippett

Millie Tucker

Susan N. Van Scyoc

Alexis Vear

Michelle Ventulett

Mary Chris Williams

Merrell Woodyard

Tiffany Wray

Paige Wright

Sharon Yokelson

INDEX

INDEX

INDEX

INDEX

INDEX

INDEX